The Black Mozart

Le Chevalier De Saint-Georges

By

Walter E. Smith

authorHOUSE®

AuthorHouse™
1663 Liberty Drive
Bloomington, IN 47403
www.authorhouse.com
Phone: 1 (800) 839-8640

Published by AuthorHouse 05/03/2016

ISBN: 978-1-4184-0796-4 (sc)
ISBN: 978-1-4184-0795-7 (e)

Library of Congress Control Number: 2004092205

Print information available on the last page.

This book is printed on acid-free paper.

Table of Contents

PREFACE

Several years ago, I was working in New York city as a teacher in an after school program to develop a Black Studies Program, when I came upon a book entitled, "Africa's Gift to America," Volume II. It was written by J.A. Rogers. Among the many characters in this well documented book was a brief biography of Joseph Bologne, Le Chevalier de Saint-Georges. I had never heard of this man. I read with great interest and surprise about this unbelievable character. I could not believe that a man could have been this talented and famous during his life-time and be so unknown today. I was so surprised and fascinated with this character that I decided to do some research. Fortunately, at the end of this book was a bibliography. Reading about Saint-Georges reminded me that I had graduated from college with a degree in French and did not know at that time that Alexandre Dumas was black. Even after graduate school, I still had not heard of him. I was twenty five years old when I found out that Alexandre Pushkin, Russia's greatest poet and considered the father of Russian literature was of black ancestry. So, it was possible to be educated and not be aware of many important facts about historical figures.

The more I discovered about Saint-Georges, the more I wanted to know. Saint-Georges was an extraordinary man living during a fascinating period in French History, 1789 to 1799, the period of The French Revolution. The fact that he was a mulatto made him even more interesting. France, at this time, had many colonies of slaves from Africa in the Caribbean Islands where he was born.

When Saint-Georges was born on the island of Guadeloupe in 1739, from a union of a wealthy white Frenchman and a slave woman called "La belle Nanon", Louis XV was the King of France; George III was the King of England, and the United States was still a colony. Saint-Georges lived before and during the French Revolution. He grew up during the Enlightenment period and the Age of Reason, a time when the intellectuals were questioning Royalty and the idea of a democratic society. His contemporaries were Voltaire, Rousseau, Diderot, Montesquieu and John Locke, some of the philosophers who criticized French society and advocated expanding more individual freedoms.

Saint-Georges was a great fencer, a composer, conductor, virtuoso, an artful equestrian, an exceptional marksman, an elegant dancer, an accomplished man of his time and one of the most important musicians in France, from 1765 until 1789. He was imitated for his style of dress and copied as a fencer. There was even a book on fencing, by Henry Angelo, who ran a famous academy in London, which used Saint-Georges as a model. He walked among Royalty, and was acquainted with many of the great men of his day, including the Duke of Orléans, the cousin of King Louis XV and the Prince of Wales, later, King George IV.

He served France as a colonel in the army during the French Revolution and made contributions that history assigned to others. Serving under him was a lieutenant colonel, Alexandre Dumas, who later became a general under Napoleon and the father of Dumas, père, the author of The Three Musketeers, The Count of Monte Cristo, and many other great works. He fought many duels, and because he was so great with the foil and so gentle as a man, he never killed anyone. He was known as a kind, gentle and generous man. His generosity was illustrated by supporting several poor families. He was mentioned in several "Mémoires"of famous men of his day. He was invited to their estates, rode and hunted with them and shared with them his love of music.

He was famous in Paris and constantly discussed by the Bourgeoisie. He conducted and performed in many concerts. He is the only man I know of with such a great resume, who is not in our contemporary history books. Today, there are web sites, records, CD's, a few books, and several biographical essays written about him. To most of you, I hurry to introduce an extraordinary man, Joseph Bologne, Le Chevalier de Saint-Georges!

The Beginning of Greatness

An elegant carriage with two regal black horses glides on cobblestone streets in Paris, approaching a building that resembles a palace. The year is 1752. The keeper opens the gate, allowing the carriage to enter. The driver climbs down quickly and opens the carriage door. A tall, handsome, apparently wealthy man disembarks first, then he helps a young, bright-eyed, handsome boy down from the carriage. The gatekeeper gasps, then quickly looks away. The wooden door opens and they enter.

"Welcome," says a proper, middle-aged man who has the air of being in charge. He is Monsieur La Boëissière and this is his school, one of the most famous fencing schools for boys in all of France and one of the most difficult to gain admittance.

"You must be Monsieur Bologne?"

"Yes, and this is my son, Joseph Bologne Saint Georges."

Monsieur Boëissière, although shocked, recovers quickly and manages very well to mask these feelings, as a man of his position and class often must. He invites M. Bologne into his larger, elegant office.

"You must realize that this is a little unusual," he says. M. Bologne, looking straight into M. La Boëissière's eyes, replies, "This is my thirteen year-old son who has been accepted into your school. I trust that he will acquire the fine education of which your school is famous. If you have any questions that you would like to ask me, please do so, for I must leave immediately. Urgent business awaits me." M. La Boëissière certainly has questions but dares not ask. He has never faced this particular type of situation before, so he simply declines to voice his concerns. M. Bologne kisses little St. Georges on his beautiful brown, mulatto cheek and quietly departs.

M. La Boëissière takes St. Georges to the courtyard and introduces him to a large group of boys. They all stare unabashedly. Some of them have servants from the French colonies and they understand, although they are surprised to see one of them here. Others have never seen a person of color. After they regain their composure, some of the boys are resentful and walk away; others approach slowly to greet St.-Georges. One of them, Lamotte, who is very short, admires how tall and strong St.-Georges appears and sees the friendliness in his eyes. Lamotte introduces himself to St.-Georges and offers to show him around.

The following day, St.-Georges begins classes with the rest of the boys. The first class is French literature. St.-Georges does well, due to his prior instruction at home. He goes from literature to science, to music, language, and dance. St.-Georges had shown a talent for the violin at an early age, so he chooses to continue. At the end of these classes, all the boys assemble in the arms room to practice fencing. La Boëissière's school is famous throughout France for its fencing program. La Boëissière's père will later become the Master of Arms of the Academy of the King, Louis XV.

After some instruction, the boys pair off. St.-Georges is matched with Roland, one of the boys who doesn't speak to him in private or in front of the instructors. Roland feels insulted, but he dares not let the instructor or M. La Boëissière see him act rudely to any other student. After all, this school is for gentlemen. St.-Georges's natural athleticism helps him to adapt quickly to fencing. Almost immediately, he gets the better of Roland. This infuriates Roland and he begins to hate

St.-Georges. Roland tells his best friend, Pierre, that one day, he will make St.-Georges pay for embarrassing him in front of the other boys.

Four years pass. St.-Georges is almost fully developed physically. He excels in all his classes, especially in fencing. He is, in fact, the best fencer at the school. Over time, he fences with the best in his school. Handily, he defeats them all. Lamotte is a fine fencer also, but not as good as St.-Georges. By now, Lamotte is his best friend. They are inseparable. This friendship will last throughout their lives.

After six years, at the age of nineteen, St.-Georges leaves the school.

Chapter I

Childhood in the Antilles.

The island of Guadeloupe was discovered by Columbus in 1493 and has been a French possession since 1635. Guadeloupe is composed of two distinct islands, separated by the Salt River. The smallest of the islands is called Grande-Terre, which is flat, compared to the larger island, Basse-Terre, which has the volcano La Soufrière. This volcano was active during the 17th and 18th centuries during the reigns of Louis XIV, XV and XVI. Guadeloupe consists of several smaller islands nearby, like La Desirade, Marie Galante and Les Saintes. Guadeloupe was a dependency of Martinique until 1775. Even today, all of these islands are still French colonies.

On the larger, beautiful tropical island of Grande-Terre, in the year 1739, a child was born. He was to play an important role in Parisian life during the 18th century. This child was born of a brief union between a slave woman of such great beauty that she was known as "La belle Nanon", (The beautiful Nanon) and a "Grand blanc" (a rich white man or an aristocrat), Monsieur Joseph Bologne, a wealthy plantation owner.

1

La belle Nanon was so beautiful that all who saw her were struck by her exotic allure. This striking woman bore M. Bologne a handsome son. Although she was then a slave, her son was not, because he was the acknowledged son of a white man who had the power to free any of his slaves.

Little Joseph Bologne Saint-Georges grew more handsome each year, spending his early childhood playing on Grande-Terre, spared of the chores that slave children had to perform. The only unusual thing about his childhood was that he was not a slave, or treated as a slave as some other mulattos were. He was also a little unusual because his skin was a little darker than most mulattos.

Saint-Georges' name at birth was Joseph Bologne, the same as his father. The name Saint-Georges was taken from the finest vessel in the harbor of Guadeloupe. This was to serve him instead of a godfather.

Roger de Beauvoir, in his novel Le Chevalier de Saint-Georges (1840), gives many details of the early life of Saint-Georges and his mother.[1] This book is considered nothing more than a fabrication in many of its tales that cannot be documented, especially about St.-Georges before he was thirteen years old. At his birth on the island, no one suspected that Saint-Georges would ever go to Paris or would become a legend. Although it was common that most aristocrats and artists to write their mémoires, Saint-Georges did not. When it was suggested later in his life that he do so, he responded modestly that he didn't feel that his life would be that important to posterity.

A more recent "biography" was written on the life of Saint-Georges titled Qui était Le Chevalier de Saint-Georges? (Who was the Chevalier de Saint-Georges?) by Odet Denys (1972). According to Denys in his Avant-Propos, his book is based on some memoirs that he found in his parents' home in

Guadeloupe after the death of his father. He claims that the inscription on these memoirs read "Mémoires sur le Chevalier de Saint-Georges" (Memoirs on the Chevalier de Saint-Georges). In his book, he does not pretend that these memoirs were written by Saint-Georges but, rather by his best friend, whom he does not identify. From all evidence, St. - Georges's father died in Paris.

A review of his book is given in the Parisian periodical L'Université Française, No. 65, September and October, 1972, by Pierre Grosclaude, who provides a most interesting and revealing comment regarding these "mémoires." He asks:

> Did the author really discover one day, in the course of a voyage to Guadeloupe, a roll of yellowed papers bearing as a title, Memoirs on the Chevalier de Saint-Georges, while rummaging in the attic of his old family residence of Pointe-à-Pitre? This manuscript was addressed, so he believed, to his paternal grandfather, in which the narrator appears to have been a very intimate friend of the Chevalier. Perhaps it is only a question of amiable and fictitious creation. Not withstanding: what is essential is that M. Odet Denys, haunted by his Antillean childhood by the figure of this strange known personage, had decided to revive him. For that reason, he at great

length and abundantly documented his tale. He drew from dossiers, from material archives, in the administrative Archives of the Minister of War, in the gazettes, newspapers and memoirs of the second half of the XVIIIth century, in the anthologies of the most diverse of authentic documents: from the best historians and before all of the contemporaries of his personage the most convincing evidences...For the remainder, that is to say, in order to supply that which in the exciting life of the Chevalier de Saint-Georges, escaped his investigations, he let his imagination run rampant, depicting him in such a manner so as not to exceed certain limits. Thus explains very neatly M. Pierre Cot in the judicious preface that he wrote from this work...[2]

Since very little authenticated information exists regarding the early years of Saint-Georges, I will occasionally quote from Denys' book, but bear in mind that I, too, doubt the authenticity of much of this information. Although it's a novel, it does make interesting reading and bridges the great gap that exists between Saint-Georges' birth until the age of 13, when his life began to be recorded. I suggest the reader regard Denys as inventive but suspect.

While Saint-Georges was still a young boy, Louis XV granted M. Bologne a large sugarcane plantation in the French part of the island of San Domingo, also called Hispañiola. This island, about the size of Ireland today, is divided into two parts, the French-speaking part is known today as Haiti. The Spanish-speaking known today as the Dominican Republic. Columbus discovered the island of Hispañiola in 1492. The city of San Domingo, was founded in 1496, and is the oldest settlement by Europeans in the western hemisphere. In a tomb in this city lay the ashes of Columbus, supposedly.

M. Bologne's plantation on Guadeloupe produced cocoa and coffee. His new plantation of sugar cane on the much larger island was more promising, as was the island itself. This island boasted the most invigorating economy of all French possessions in America or in Asia.

On the much larger island of San Domingo, Saint-Georges found a very different atmosphere. There were many more slaves, the slave masters there were more cruel. Slavery on this island, in general, was worse than in the American colonies. The French slave owners were brutal and inhumane. The slaves were housed like animals, worked harder than animals, and fed so little that they slowly starved to death. A NEGRO CODE was passed in 1685, authorizing whipping. The code number of lashes was set at 39. Later, it was changed to 50. The colonists paid no attention to the CODE and often whipped slaves to death. Animals were treated better and were fed to live a long life, but not the slaves.

There was no end to the imagination of the slave traders, and owners. Even the prisoners in French Guiana, made famous by the story of Papillon, were treated better. They could grow their own food, live separately, and had free time to do as they wished. The treatment of the slaves was a perfect example of an economy based on slave labor.

Here, the slaves were driven to homicidal mania. Poison was the method of choice. C.L.R. James, in his book, The Black Jacobins, gives a vivid accounting of this homicidal mania.

> A mistress would poison a rival to retain the valuable affections of her inconstant owner. A discarded mistress would poison master, wife, children and slaves. A slave robbed of his wife by one of his masters would poison him, and this was one of the most frequent causes of poisoning. If a planter conceived a passion for a young slave, her mother would poison his wife with the idea of placing her daughter at the head of the household. The slaves would poison the younger children of a master in order to ensure the plantation succeeding to one son. By this means, they prevented the plantation being broken up and the gang dispersed. On certain plantations the slaves decimated their number by poisoning so as to keep the number of slaves small and prevent their masters embarking on larger schemes which would increase the work. For this reason,

a slave would poison his wife, another would poison his children, and a Negro nurse declared in court that for years she had poisoned every child that she brought into the world. Nurses employed in hospitals poisoned sick soldiers to rid themselves of unpleasant work. The slaves would even poison the property of a master whom they loved. He was going away; they poisoned cows, horses and mules, the plantation was thrown into disorder, and the beloved master was compelled to remain. The most dreadful of all this cold-blooded murder was, however, the jaw-sickness--a disease, which attacked children only, in the first few days of their existence. Their jaws were closed to such an extent that it was impossible to open them and to get anything down, with the result that they died of hunger. It was not a natural disease and never attacked children delivered by white women. The Negro midwives alone could cause it, and it is believed that they performed some simple operation on the newly born child which resulted in the jaw sickness. Whatever the

method this disease caused the
death of nearly one third of the
children born on the plantations.[3]

It was just amazing how all of this brutality and barbarity could flourish on this beautiful island of coconut trees, palm trees and soft breezes! But it did!

This behavior seems to have been unique to San Domingo. I have never read or heard of this kind of madness in North America, which had many more slaves.

The madness continued for one hundred and fifty years, until the slaves began to revolt. This will be described in greater detail later.

Monsieur Bologne decided to take his family to Paris. It is not clear why he left, but witnessing this nightmare, which was contrary to his nature, must have played a part. Saint-Georges was 10 years old when they left the beautiful island that, he felt, without slavery would have been his paradise.

Saint-Georges was too young to anticipate his reception in a world completely dominated and numbered by whites like his father. He probably did not realize that being the son of a black woman would follow him all his life. This would have been a great deal to think about for a 10-year-old. And certainly neither his father nor his mother could have realized that fate would designate Saint-Georges a great man of the 18th century. For who knows what would have happened to Saint-Georges had his father remained on the island? He could have become more and more bitter and might have behaved like Toussaint L'Ouverture, or he could have taken advantage of his position and became an aristocratic mulatto and a slave owner, like many other mulattos.

Roger de Beauvoir, in his novel Le Chevalier de Saint-Georges, states that Saint-Georges knew Toussaint as a boy and had a fight with him. This was possible since the two boys were about the same age. Many years later, when Saint-Georges visited the island of San Domingo, he probably did meet Toussaint, but this time they were both great and well-known men.[4]

Also, according to Roger de Beauvoir, Saint-Georges and his mother were not taken to France by M. Bologne. Rather he supposedly ran away to Paris from the island. This certainly was not the case. Imagine a 10 year-old or in M. de Beauvoir's novel, a 13 year-old mulatto boy, getting all the way to Paris alone. In Beauvoir's novel, we later find Saint-Georges at 21 years of age, refined, and rather wealthy. With no plausible explanation of how he attained such a complete education and money.

I will occasionally refer to M. de Beauvoir's novel since there are many documented facts in it. Also, maybe one can see how history became history and facts became facts. As G. Orwell convinced us, it all depends on who's writing it. After Saint-Georges' arrival in Paris, we can more reliably document his evolution.

There were different opinions as to St.-Georges' birth date. There was a consensus, even mentioned as fact by almost all who wrote about Saint-Georges, that he was born on December 25, 1745. Only Gaston Bourgeois in his <u>Le Chevalier de Saint Georges Inexactitudes Commise Par Ses Biographes in 1949</u> (Inaccuracies Committed by his Biographers) suggests that Saint-Georges was born between 1738 and 1739.[5] Odet Denys, who has written the only complete biography of Saint-Georges since Roger de Beauvoir, claiming it to be the most accurate, gives Saint-Georges' birthday as 1739. It is now accepted that he was born in 1739.

There is also disagreement as to who his father was and the spelling of the surname Bologne. Roger de Beauvoir in his novel does not even mention the father of Saint-Georges, until Saint-Georges is a grown man, famous and rich, living in Paris. According to most sources, his father was Jean-Nicholas de Boulogne or Boullongne, adviser to the King in his Parliament of Metz, Intendant of Finances in May, 1744, and on the 25th of August, 1757, named Controller General of Finances of his Majesty, that is to say, Secretary of State of Finances. Again, according to Gaston Bourgeois, Saint-Georges' father was of the branch of Boullongne of Beauvaisis, who had a common origin with the illustrious Boullongne painters of Paris. Further, his first name was Guillaume-Pierre, born at Orléans on the 17th of June, 1770. And again, I use as my main source of information for the early years of Saint-Georges Odet Denys' biography. He says that Saint-Georges' father was Monsieur Bologne Saint-Georges, Gentleman of the Chamber of the King.

According to Allan Bradley, St. Georges' father was George de Bologne St. Georges.[6] He says that the Bologne family traced its ancestry to Bologne, Italy, hence the family name. George Bologne married Elizabeth-Françoise Jeanne Mérican on September 8, 1739. They had a daughter, Elizabeth, born on January 21, 1740, making St.-Georges one year older than his half-sister. She lived in Paris during St.-Georges' lifetime. Of course, he had to have known her because they came over on the same ship. They lived for a time in the same house. This is a missing and mysterious part of his life that no biographer has tried to treat. It would be so interesting to know some factual details of their adult relationship. What did she think of her older brother who was bigger than life in the great city of Paris? Did she deny him, fearing her status might be diminished? I would love to know the answers.

Roger de Beauvoir presents pages and pages of graphic details, which, according to all my sources, must have been pure invention. But remember, his is a historical novel. Also, remember that before the publication of Denys' biography in 1972, Roger de Beauvoir's novel was the only complete book about Saint-Georges, which probably accounts for the other biographers repeating these unsubstantiated "facts".

---

[1] Beauvoir, Roger de- Le Chevalier de Saint-Georges Paris, 1840 H.L. Delloye 2nd Ed. n.p.

[2] Grosclaude, Pierre- L'Université Française, No. 65 September and October- Paris, 1972

[3] James, C.L.R.—The Black Jacobins, Random House, Inc. 1963 p.16

[4] Beauvoir, Roger de

[5] Bourgeois, Gaston n.p.

[6] Bradley, Allan: Le Chevalier de Saint-Georges (1748-1799)

Chapter II

Becoming a Gentleman in Paris

The Bologne family arrived in Paris around 1749. They moved into a luxury house in one of the finer neighborhoods. St.-Georges and La belle Nanon must have been shocked by the new sights that were so different from the island. The climate made the biggest difference. Paris had cobbled stone streets that made the horses hoofs and carriage wheels sound loud. The elegant carriages were very different from the ones in Guadeloupe, although they did have a few fine ones there, too. However, the weather made the covered ones too hot in Guadeloupe, whereas in Paris, they needed them for the cold, damp weather. In Guadeloupe, the houses were wood-framed with much land and greenery between. The next house or farm could not be seen without a long ride. In Paris, except for the very rich, people lived in apartments.

Detail of Record

The cultural differences were extreme. Paris had its operas, concert halls, ice-skating rinks and huge parties held by the rich and noble classes. Many of the rich in Paris inherited their money. Others made money, but did not get their hands dirty. Many made money from the slave trade but did not have to witness its brutality and inhumanity. The rich in the islands were managers or owners of great estates and were in direct contact with their businesses of raising cocoa and sugarcane and the buying and selling of slaves. They did not have the operas, concerts, and the many distractions of the rich in Paris. Maybe they were so brutal because they didn't have the distractions of Paris. They had too much time on their hands to think of new ways to punish their slaves.

This new life presented great changes and adjustments for the Bologne family, especially St.-Georges, la belle Nanon and little Elizabeth.

For the next three years, I have no information about St.-Georges's life, or La belle Nanon's, or what M. Bologne did for business or pleasure. Here we can realistically imagine Saint-Georges absorbing the Parisian life and becoming more French than Antillean, and more Parisian, as Parisians considered themselves different and better than other French people, as they do today.

From age thirteen, until his death, much of Saint-Georges' public life can be documented with reasonable accuracy. Since he was such an extraordinary and sometimes controversial figure, there are still different versions of some incidents in his life; I will try to give the version I found to be more plausible.

At the age of thirteen, he was boarded at the school of La Boëssière, where he received the sort of education that a rich father could provide. He was busy every morning in earnest study of the masters of literature, science, music, language and dance. The rest of the day was spent in the weapons room. At age fifteen, he vanquished the strongest fencers; at the age of seventeen, he had acquired an agility of movement which baffled the great fencing masters. It was in 1754, when Saint-Georges was about fifteen years old and making his mark as a fencer, that France saw the birth of the heir to the throne. On August 23, 1754, a son was born to Louis XV, who would later become King Louis XVI.

By the age of nineteen, Saint-Georges had developed a fine athletic body. He had great strength, agility and speed. He excelled in every sport and physical endeavor. He was the most graceful and proficient fencer; a great runner and a marvelous horse-back rider. He was known to ride the most difficult horses bareback better than most with a saddle. In the winter, when the Seine was frozen, people would gather to watch him ice skate with the same grace as Saint-Georges, the fencer and dancer. As a marksman with a pistol, he rarely missed the target. There had never been a man so gifted physically.

At an early age, he showed a great interest in music and, as in most endeavors which he pursued, he excelled. Because of his obvious talent, he became a student of Jean-Marie Leclair.

He studied the violin and became very accomplished in a short time. Other musicians were amazed at his talent and marveled at how he mastered the difficult instrument in such a short time. But the art in which he surpassed his contemporaries and predecessors, was fencing.

The greatest accolade regarding Saint-Georges the fencer comes from the fencing master himself. La Boëssière, in his Traité de L'Art Des Armes (Treatise on the Art of Fencing) proclaimed that:

Saint-Georges was endowed with extraordinary strengths, with extraordinary vigor. Lively, flexible, slender, he was astonishing by his alertness. No one ever in the art of fencing displayed more grace, more steadiness. He had superb style, his hand held up to the highest, rendered him always master of the weak side of his adversary; his left foot, solidly planted, never wavered, and his right leg remained constantly perpendicular. This combination of skills provided him with that coolness which permitted him to raise himself up at the same time to recover immediately with the swiftness of a flash of lightning.

He was admired particularly in his manner of shadow-fencing; he was so sure of his skills that he instinctively touched on both sides and frankly, while observing all the principles. His quarteⁱ on the weapons were especially astonishing. He was even more surprising when the sword engaged inside; he would find himself at a

ⁱblade up and to the inside, wrist supinated

good reach and en garde[ii] for the attack. He recommended not to shake or move, taking it upon himself not to make any false move before starting. If by chance he took the least time, the blow did not count. He executed the blow of quarte sur les armes[iii] with such precision, touching and repassing his foil in his left hand with so much quickness that the defender would not have the time to meet the iron for the parry[iv].

One can imagine what a fencer with such speed can do, who can call his thrust beforehand or at will, from a far-reaching range!

Who always stood apart with one of the most imposing guards. If one wished to take his sword, one found nothing. His point had such lightness that one could not feel it. If unfortunately one wished to loose one's temper, he was stopped thrust before his feet had touched the ground; finally one dared not attempt anything. The straight blows, the disengagement

[ii]en garde: the stance that fencers assume when preparing to fence

[iii]obsolete

[iv]a defensive action made by deflecting the opponent's attack

17

succeeded one another and overpowered you.

Managing his speed well, he would use it with a sure blow. Against an adversary who was skilled in parrying well, he only fenced after having fait un temp^v, in order to pass a blow of lightness at the moment when one touched bladed. It is known that in fencing on the bend, however adept that one is, one can withdraw too late, and be parried; in consequence, one must try to squeeze, and to interrupt the bend at anytime whatever: this is what Saint-Georges used to execute with great precision. It was impossible to match him blow for blow, however determine one might be.

He was in control at all times, and never fenced without assuring himself of a sword.

If he realized that he might be opposed with unethical tricks, the sword was upset by crossings, and clashing so vigorously and so elastic, that the arms were broken from it. Let one judge by these hardy developments which would

---

^{v}Time interval during which the response can be effected by retaining its priority.

follow, as well as the coup de temps[vi] and the stop thrusts which followed each other like streaks of lightning.

He used to reserve for the strongest the stop thrust and the coup de temps, saving for himself only the parry and the riposte[vii], and no one could touch him. In this exercise where he displayed all the grace and all the skills that nature had given him, he would surprise the spectators.

As one sees him, Saint-Georges had arrived at an ideal perfection, which up to the present has not yet been attained by anyone. One can say that his epoch was the apex of the art of fencing. Masters and students distinguished themselves alike in this by the same perfection, although to lesser degrees.

One had arrived at such suppleness of movements, one had so light and so reserved a hand that one would not put his sword into the body of the adversary, that one wished to put it into. Their intention was to lay each other out

[vi]when a stop hit arrives at least one fencing time before the original attack
[vii]an attack made immediately after a party of the opponent's attack

under the pale and trembling light of a street lantern.[1]

La Boëssière also said about Saint-Georges that: Racine created Phèdre and I created Saint-Georges, praise a little excessive, but which confirms however a reputation that all the fencers of the period have acknowledged unchangeable.

Saint-Georges left M. de La Boëssière at the age of nineteen.

Because of M. Bologne's position as a gentleman, his son, in spite of his color, was able to enter the high society as a gentleman. He frequented the well-known salons of the time, where he encountered the rich and famous of Paris. He was readily accepted. His excellent education and his charming manners brought him much success. His handsome body and his sensuous heart certainly aided him in his association with the ladies of his class. The combination of his physique, his gentleness, his goodness, his charm; made him irresistible to women. Women liked him immediately and his success with them became legendary.

Shortly after he left M. de La Boëssière's school, he entered the Company of the Musketeers. Yet, the prejudices against men of color, and the cutting remarks of his comrades forced him to resign.

Gaston Bourgeois in his <u>Le Chevalier De Saint-Georges, Inexactitudes Commises Par Ses Biographes</u>, said that Saint-Georges could not have entered the Musketeers because:

All the musketeers were gentlemen; and the cadets from the greatest families prided themselves in serving in this elite company. Well, Saint-Georges was not of noble 'race'.[2]

Around this same time, he was also appointed esquire to the Duchess of Orléans, the wife of the brother of King Louis XVI. While serving in this position, he gained a powerful friend and protector in the Duke of Orléans. After the death of the Duke, his friendly relations continued with his son, the Duke of Chartres.

Although there is some controversy about Saint-Georges having been a Musketeer, it is certain that about the same time when he was allegedly in and out of the Musketeers, he was a Soldier of the Guard of the King. Saint-Georges was about sixteen years old at that time. His tenure in the Royal Guard lasted for about 5 years. During these years Louis XV and Mme de Pompadour ruled over the Court at Versailles. Later, under Louis XVI, Saint-Georges would play his role in the social life and intrigues of Louis XVI and Marie Antoinette.

Mme de Pompadour was born Jeanne Antoinette Poisson in Paris in 1721, the daughter of a middle class family. When she was four years old, in 1725, her father, Francois Poisson, was forced to leave France because of a black market scandal and to escape his creditors. In France at that time, and in most of Europe, if people owed money and could not pay, they could be put in debtors jail. By the time she was nine years old, her mother insisted on giving her the best possible education so that little Jeanne could marry a rich man. For example, she was given voice lessons and elocution by the best teachers. Jeanne acquired the kind of education that all rich people in Europe gave their children. The money for this education was provided for by her mother's lover, Charles Le Normant de Tournehem. Some historians list him as her step-father.

When she reached the age of twenty-three, in 1741, an arrangement was made for her to marry a nobleman, Charles Guillaume le Normant d' Étioles. That same year, she gave birth to a daughter, Alexandrine. Shortly after, she began planning to get into the most exclusive circles of society. She entertained a great deal in her Château d' Étioles. Men like Voltaire and Montesquieu were her guests. She became so well known for her entertaining that even the King, Louis XV, heard of her and actually met her at a ball in 1745. He was very impressed with this young lady.

After the death of his mistress, the Duchess of Chateauroux, the King chose Jeanne to be his next mistress. First, he installed her in a room in his palace; she was given lessons in court etiquette to prepare her for court life. Second, in 1745, she was legally separated from her husband. The King gave her the title of the Marquise de Pompadour on July 7, 1745

She spent most of her time entertaining the King with many parties and suppers. The Marquise became widely known as a patron of the arts and literature. This is how she came to know Saint-Georges, who was himself becoming well known for his musical talents.

Years later, after she could no longer perform her duties as a mistress to the King, the lovers' relationship thereafter, was based on friendship. He gave her the highest honor he could bestow, naming her a duchess. The King remained devoted to her until her death. Most women, especially those not of noble birth, during this period had limited roles to play in society.

Yet, Madame de Pompadour surpassed the traditional role and became a woman of great power and influence.

M. de Bologne, Saint-Georges' father, died shortly after his son had completed his studies and training at the school of M. de La Boëssière. Saint-Georges was in his early twenties. The exact date of his father's death is uncertain.

Upon his death, M. De Bologne left his fortune to La belle Nanon. To Saint-Georges he left a yearly income of about 8000 francs. According to Henry Angelo, he left the rest of his immense fortune to a daughter by a Creole woman. There was no mention of his legal wife. This reference to a daughter by a Creole woman was an assumption made by Angelo, made by the fact that St.-Georges was a Creole. There is only one legal reference made to the daughter. According to the register of the "Bénéfices d'inventaires" of Paris, 1775, a girl named Elizabeth Bénédictine de Bologne Saint-Georges is listed,

Saint-Georges became what was considered a great lover, admired by most men and loved by many women. These women didn't seem to mind his wooly hair and dark skin. His many other exceptional qualities over-shadowed these characteristics that some would have considered handicaps in the all-white aristocratic society. The fact that he was also an illegitimate child also didn't seem to deter the women of the day. Although Saint-Georges boasted of many sexual conquests, there seems to be only one lengthy, detailed account of his prowess and that was with his first love. I cannot verify this account but it was allegedly among the memoirs upon which Denys based his book.

Young Saint-Georges in 1768

When St.-Georges was twenty years old, he had his first love with an eighteen-year-old. He had been introduced to her in a salon. They danced together and St.-Georges was very attracted to her, but he had no idea how she felt about him.

One day during a hunting party, they found themselves next to each other. Each hunter had been placed next to a young person whom he liked. Suddenly, they found themselves alone. He stared at her with love in his eyes. She seemed shy, but he noticed that her eyes were receptive. After a few minutes, he asked her if he could kiss her. Before she could answer, their lips touched gently in a very sweet kiss. They sat next to a small sand dune and she poured sand on his hand. Their fingers intertwined and he softly kissed her pretty face, which was red with emotion. They heard the birds singing as though celebrating those precious moments. She didn't seem to notice his color nor did he notice hers at that moment. Although her white skin contrasted with his brown color, it was not an issue. It was all emotion of two young people falling in love. He had never kissed a European but that was not the reason for his pleasure. They were just two human beings who loved each other. All the prejudices did not exist for them.

He saw her again in Paris, more smitten than ever. He listened intently to her every word. At that time, some people would pay their valets and servants to take notes and to help arrange secret meetings. They were above all that.

One of St.-Georges' friends, a young officer, owned a house in a very respectable neighborhood. The officer was away for a time. The lovers agreed to meet there. She would pretend to visit some of her lady friends. She would quickly excuse herself from them and hurry to see him.

It was the happiest time of his short life. Everything was new. Her shyness slowly disappeared as they became closer. Her innocence and tenderness made him even happier. They would hold each other seemingly possessed. Nothing in the world was as pleasurable as when two people loved each other boundlessly.

Summer vacations separated them so she wrote him youthful, beautiful love letters. A few years later, a jealous woman discovered them in his house and destroyed them.

They loved each other for several years with all the power and passion that two people could feel. But in spite of everything, it could not last. Barriers were erected between them. He was a nobleman, but a nobleman of color, and a bastard.

Her father and two brothers came to St.-Georges and told him clearly and emphatically that he could not see her again. If he persisted, they would be forced to bring great harm to him, socially as well as physically. They did not wish to have grand-children of an "inferior" race. They said that it would be an embarrassment to the family to have him as a family member. They absolutely could not continue their illicit affair.

A short time later, she was married off to the son of a wealthy nobleman. St.-Georges hid behind a column of the church and watched her leave on someone else's arm. What began as the best time of his life, ended as the worst. He went home despondent, beyond repair.

Later, he saw her in society, but they never spoke. It was a painful silence. Serving all of his life, he had a special place in his heart for her. First love endures. He would often take out a small locket that she had given him and he felt grateful for having shared such great pleasure even though there were still vestiges of pain.

This painful and disappointing first love affair left a great scar on Saint-Georges. He was never the same with women after that, although he was loving, tender, and thoughtful. This affair may account for the fact that Saint-Georges went from one woman to another and loved many, but was never again in love.

I did have amorous or
gallant adventures; it was however
in place of the home I dreamed of
having with the only woman that
I've really loved. I followed my

destiny. If I flew from one woman
to another, it was not my fault.[3]

Although Saint-Georges loved women and left them,
the only regret women had was his leaving, because he was
far from cruel while loving them. He was loved greatly for
his tenderness, warmth and his sincere respect for all women.
What more could they ask from him except an eternity of it?
There was a profound gratitude to have loved him. In this, he
felt and showed a deep gratitude for having been loved as a
man, regardless of his color.

With his inheritance, his many attributes, and great
charm, Saint-Georges burst upon the society of Paris. He was
welcomed in the highest circles and was indeed treated like the
gentleman he was.

During the 17th, 18th and 19th centuries, there were
many salons. Some became more famous and were frequented
by the most notable of the day. At these salons, the rich, the
artists, men and women of letters congregated and socialized.
To be invited to certain salons was very prestigious. Saint-
Georges frequented the salon of La Marquise de Champonas,
who was famous for the choice of people invited to her soirées.
Saint-Georges was a man of fashion and his dress was imitated.
Young people followed him and sought his company even for
a brief moment of conversation. He was seen in all the elegant
places, even in the Royal Palaces.

Many evenings after the concerts, Saint-Georges
would walk along the most popular boulevards. Other times
he would ride in his fine carriage. He was always recognized
and acknowledged. He was one of the favorites of the Parisian
crowd. The women of the lower class smiled; the young women
blew kisses to him.

Saint-Georges was invited to all of the celebrations and was constantly in demand to dine at the homes of people of the highest social rank.

As welcomed as Saint-Georges was in most circles, there were those who only accepted him superficially. He felt it sometimes when he was not welcome by all when attending some social function. Saint-Georges concluded that, since he had on occasion been subtly made aware that he was a gentleman, but of color, he had to be a little more polite than other gentleman toward his peers as well as to the man on the street or he might be open to racial repercussions. After all, even though he was a gentleman, his ancestors were black slaves. France, at this time still was in the slavery business in the two islands of Saint-Georges' childhood, as well as in other French colonies. He understood this early. Was a person of color ever really accepted by whites in this hierarchical society? Some people were big enough and secure enough to accept another person as a human being. Plus, Saint-Georges made every party or occasion much more enjoyable. Wasn't Saint-Georges an extremely talented man, a man of clever wit, and a pleasure to behold and a pleasure to love? Why then could he not be accepted as a peer, a man equal as they?

Some took great pride in being Saint-Georges' protector, and he accepted this, but he realized all the time what the relationship between the protector and the protected was really about.

In every memoir, in every article, indeed in all my research, Saint-Georges was always referred to as the mulatto, never just Saint-Georges, the fencer, the musician, etc.

There was clearly this arrogance of superiority shown by some, but at the same time, the majority appreciated and lauded his works in France and in many other countries, especially England. These became his true admirers. His color didn't seem to matter to them, only his great contributions to French life and the French pleasures. His success and talent as a violinist and as a composer were especially lauded by the best French musicians and composers of the day, like Gossec, Laurencie, Le Clerc and many others.

Although some biographers suggested that Saint-Georges was ugly, most people spoke of how handsome he was. Those who spoke of him as ugly, were in the minority. Was it an opinion or prejudice and jealousy? It was stated by Bachaumont that "...he is a valorous champion of love and was sought out by all the ladies aware of his marvelous talent, in spite of the ugliness of his face."[4] Another reference to Saint-Georges' face was from H. Angelo who in recounting the story of a painting of Saint-Georges said that when Angelo's mother inquired of Saint-Georges if the painting in question of him was a good likeness, Saint-Georges replied, "Oh, madame, it is so resembling that it is ugly."[5] So many other contemporaries, on the contrary spoke of Saint-Georges as being extremely handsome. That he had a well-built body presented no controversy. One of the few portraits still available painted by Brown, an American artist shows his face to be handsome. It is suggested that since Saint-Georges' features were not white features and that in his society as well as today's, the standard of beauty is of white features- - thin lips, narrow nose, etc.

It is interesting how many controversies regarding Saint-Georges' exploits survived. History of course is interpreted by the historian, not always by the facts. A story depends on the storyteller. At several events that took place involving Saint-Georges, there were many people present who saw the events too differently; sometimes even the victor in a fencing duel was disputed.

C.L.R. James in his book, The Black Jacobins on the life of Toussaint L'Ouverture, on the subject of history and historians said:

> The writing of history becomes ever more difficult. The power of God or the weakness of man, Christianity or the divine right of kings to govern wrong, can easily be made responsible for the downfall of states and the birth of new societies. Such elementary conceptions lend themselves willingly to narrative treatment and from Tacitus to Macaulay, from Thucydides to Green, the traditionally famous historians have been more artist than scientist: they wrote so well because they saw so little. Today, by a natural reaction we tend to a personification of the social forces, great men being merely or nearly instruments in the hands of economic destiny. As so often the truth does not lie in between. Great men make history, but only such history as it is possible for them to make. Their freedom of achievement is limited by the necessities of their environment. To portray the

limits of those necessities and the
realization, complete or partial,
of all possibilities, that is the true
business of the historian.[6]

La belle Nanon lived with Saint-Georges in seclusion in his fine house, but not as his mother. The few people who saw her, thought of her as a house servant. She did not mind but St.-Georges regretted it very much. What else could he do?

It was said by J.A. Rogers that Saint-Georges did indeed take his mother into the most brilliant salons, he presented her to his aristocratic friends, letting it be quietly known that whoever attempted to snub her would in turn be snubbed by him. "Who refuses her refuses me," he said.[7] I found no evidence of this and it is very unlikely that Saint-Georges could have done so. It is unlikely so, for many reasons, especially since Saint-Georges himself was not immune from being snubbed, as he occasionally was.

Saint-Georges had many encounters with adversaries, enemies and sometimes just plain robbers. One night Saint-Georges and a friend were walking down the street after attending a party when they were attacked by six men. Saint-Georges and his friend fought off the attackers. A pistol was fired and St.-Georges was slightly wounded and had a few bruises. The police arrested three of the attackers. When the Duke of Orléans, cousin of the King and protector and friend of St.-Georges heard of this attack, he demanded that the police chief investigate. A day later, the Duke was asked not to meddle in this affair. The attackers were policemen. It was understood by the Duke and St.-Georges that he had a powerful enemy, but they did not know who it was or why St.-Georges was attacked.

Saint-Georges received many letters of condolences regarding his attack and minor wounds. The news of this affair traveled rapidly among society and brought him more fame and a great deal of sympathy from the ladies. He was viewed as adventurous, courageous and heroic. He was invited to even more salons and fêtes. Everyone wanted to talk to him, to hear of the adventures first hand. When walking in the streets, he was stared at and people whispered his name. Jean de Beauvoir who knew St.-Georges wrote:

> As soon as St.-Georges appeared in any circle, a murmur, to which all had long been accustomed, circulated through the room. They recognized him; and the expression of an unforgettable joy shone on his handsome brown face. The women, on seeing him, had the appearance of hiding behind their fans, as if to convey a secret to one another, while the men, the most distinguished in nobility, and intelligence, came forward to shake his hand. In an instant he had become the lion of the assembly.[8]

Lamotte, St.-Georges' best friend, believed that some of the students from La Boëssière's school still held a grudge against him, especially Roland and Pierre. Roland had been defeated in a match when they were at the school and felt humiliated that a mulatto could get the better of him. It was to

Pierre, his best friend that he declared that he would make St.-Georges pay for this embarrassment. St.- Georges was never aware of Roland's declaration and probably thought of the match as only a fencing match between students.

Saint-Georges continued enjoying the pleasurable life until 1766, when he began turning more towards his musical talents and began studying composition under Francois Joseph Gossec (1734- 1829). At about the same time, a memorable event took place in the life of Saint-Georges that has been mentioned in many memoirs. This event was the encounter between Saint-Georges and Gian Guiseppe Faldoni.

Guiseppe's father, Andreas, was a famous fencing master in Italy. He operated a famous fencing school at Leghorn, Italy. He became famous for developing excellent fencers and for his own prowess with the foil. His son Guiseppe was born in 1739, the same year as Saint-Georges, but of course under very different circumstances. Guiseppe's father, known as one of the first fencers in Italy, taught his son well and Guiseppe, having great natural talent, as was the case with Saint-Georges, developed into a great fencer. In 1759, Guiseppe, who was better known as Faldoni, made a successful tour through Italy. No one was able to defeat him nor give him a very competitive match. In 1761, he had a difference with a lieutenant of the Tuscan regiment. The lieutenant was a very good fencer and he attacked Faldoni on a public street, for what reason was not clear. Faldoni was surprised at his boldness and gave him four quick hits with his foil. This would have killed any man, but the lieutenant was still standing and showing no blood. What Faldoni did not know was that the lieutenant was carrying mail under his shirt. Faldoni decided to finish him with a hit in the neck but he was prevented by two army officers who stepped in to separate them. This move saved the foolish lieutenant's life.

In 1763, Guiseppe went to Rome, accompanied by the renowned French fencer, Monsieur Delliser. He fenced in a public academy with Major Ruggero de Rocco Picolomini, one of the first fencers in Italy, who was at that time in the service of his majesty the King of Poland. They made four assaults (attacks), in which Faldoni made the first figure (hit). After that match, the other masters would not fence with him.

In 1764 Monsieur Delliser invited him to France, for the purpose of having a match with a French fencing master at Marseilles, who had a large wager with him on who would make the first six hits. This wager was won by Faldoni, and the money was paid. He then proceeded to Lyon, where he arrived in June, and Monsieur Delliser introduced him to a fencing master, called Simon who would advise him on how to proceed with his quest to prove that he was the best fencer.

He was advised to go to Paris, and to invite in a public academy Monsieur Saint-Georges, whom the French believed the only fencer in France that could stand before him. Accordingly, in the year 1766, he went to Paris, and was presented to Monsieur Saint-Georges, by Monsieur Lewis Delavoiner, professor of chemistry, with whom he became acquainted in Leghorn. Monsieur Saint-Georges refused to fence with him on learning he was an Italian. Faldoni then went around to all the schools in Paris, where he had ever day assaults with different masters and their prévots (assistant fencing masters), and beat them all, of which he received certificates in writing. All the masters in a body went to Saint-Georges, representing to him the necessity of his fencing with him; otherwise, they said, this Italian will boast of having beaten all the masters and assailants in Paris. Saint-Georges then determined to have and assault with him, and a meeting was given on the 8th of September, 1766, where there were several hundred spectators, nobility, etc. several masters had come for that purpose from Lyon and other parts of France, and these together with Paris masters, were placed in the third seats round the hall.[9]

The following is an abstract of a letter which Faldoni writes to his father, dated 9th of September, 1766.

I have at last finished all my assaults in Paris with one that I made yesterday with the strongest fencer in France, and truly I cannot do less than confess that I don't believe that an equal fencer is now living. But the success I have now met has been so brilliant and as much as I could wish before such a famous and powerful fencer, that I shall briefly tell you that I gave him the first two hits. I received the third, then gave him the fourth, which was as straight thrust, and was judged the finest attack in the whole assault; I again was touched with the fifth, and gave him the sixth, which was the last. I cannot describe to you the congratulations and compliments I received from all the nobility and masters; and they assured me that Paris had never seen such an assault before. The name of the man is Saint-Georges, and they believe him to be the first swordsman in Europe, and truly his thrusts are as lightning. He has a very long lunge and his passades are presqu' impénétrables (almost impenetrable). I made a memorial to the King to open a school at Lyon under my own name.[10]

The memorial was immediately granted, and in November, he made his appearance through Lyon's streets as a public master, wearing a sword-cane, and a distinction, feathers to his hat, when he opened a school in his name.[11]

    Controversy exists about who won the match, even from the spectators who recorded this event in their memoirs. Some say Saint-Georges was the victor, others say Faldoni. Still others considered it a draw. About this event, I cannot resolve the controversy. The friends of Saint-Georges supported that he could have won the match without being touched.

    I find the ironies in life fascinating. I find it so interesting and fascinating that Saint-Georges and Faldoni, born the same year under such adverse circumstances, thousands of miles apart found themselves many years later in the historic city of Paris engaged in a memorable fencing match. That Saint-Georges would have been a slave had his father been some other white man, causes one to stop and reflect on how easily this entire story could not have been. Maybe fate brought Saint-Georges to his glory and the two great fencers together.

    An anecdote related by Thiébault is perhaps worth repeating for those who have not read his Mémoires:

> Saint-Georges was one day watching a game of tennis. Among the players was a young noble, in the household of the King, a newcomer to Paris. Turning suddenly, he beheld, against the net, the face of the great mulatto. In a fit of youthful impertinence or insanity, he threw the ball at the Chevalier's nose. A challenge from Saint-Georges appeared to

amuse him immensely. He was somewhat sobered however, when his friends informed him that he was already as good as dead; and they proceeded to enlighten him as to whom Saint-Georges was.

At the meeting he said to Saint-Georges: 'Sir, I cannot defend my life against you; but I can play you for it. Here are two pistols; only one is loaded; we will select them at hazard and fire point-blank at the same moment. The lucky man will blow out the other's brains; but chance will decide.' After this Saint-Georges was willing to listen to his seconds, and the younger man apologized.[12]

---

[1]La Bössière: Traité de l' Art des Armes, Paris 1818 pp. 56-59
[2]Gaston, Bourgeois: Le Chevalier de Saint-Georges, Inexactitudes Commises Par Ses Biographes 1949 Paris n.p.
[3]Denys, Odet
[4]Bachaumont, May 1, 1977 Vol. XIV pp. 42-45
[5]Angelo, Henry: Angelo's Pic-Nick of Table Talk London, 1834 pp. 21-25
[6]James, C.L.R.
[7]Rogers, J.A. World's Great Men of Color Vol. II
[8]Beauvoir, Jean de: Le Chevalier de Saint-Georges, 2 vols Paris 1890
[9]Angelo: The Reminiscences of Henry Angelo, pp. 398-399 Paris 1830
[10]Faldoni, Guiseppe: Mémoires n.p. n.d.
[11]Thiébault-Paul-Charles Francois; Mémoires 1816 n.p.
[12]Thiébault+Paul-Charles Francois: Mémoires n.d. n.p.

Henry Angelo, Fencing Master in London, 1790

Chapter III

Saint-Georges The Composer, Conductor and Musician

Saint-Georges had studied violin with Jean-Marie Leclair (1697-1764) in his youth at La Boëssière's school and had become quite proficient with this instrument. Regarding Leclair, Marc Pincherle in his L'Influence de Leclair (The Influence of Leclair) says:

> For those who look at the panorama of French Music from a certain distance in the first half of the eighteenth century, the face of Leclair does not distinguish itself at first with much importance. Among most lovers of music, his name is far from bringing up the same cries of admiration as that of François Couperin for example.

And yet his action, in depth was to be rich and varied.

One strange thing is that what we know the least about is his activity as a professor. Of the many students that he taught we only know a few by their names, among the first class virtuosos, Dauvergne l'Abbé the son, probably Gaviniès and the Chevalier de Saint-Georges; on a less brilliant level, Mahoni who was called le Breton, author of a chacune (a kind of dance music) and of small number which are found in the collections of the time...[1]

Leclair had produced a violinist who was to become one of the best of his time. With background well established, in 1766 as I previously stated, Saint-Georges began studying composition under Joseph Gossec.

Gossec came to Paris in 1751 and was introduced to La Pouplinière, a wealthy amateur, who made him conductor of his private orchestra. It was not long after Saint-Georges began studying with Gossec before he recognized Saint-Georges' talent and admired him very much as a person, as well as a musician. He admired Saint-Georges so much that in the same year, 1766 that Saint-Georges was studying with him, he dedicated one of his works to Saint-Georges, Opus IX, six trios for two violins and bass. This was very unusual for a composer to do at this time. It was common for composers during the sixties (1760's) to dedicate works to their powerful patrons rather than to their colleagues. Gossec said in his dedication:

> To Monsieur de Saint-Georges, Esquire, Gendarme of the King's Guard. Monsieur,
>
> The great reputation that you have acquired through your talents and the favorable reception that you give to artists have made me take the liberty to dedicate to you this work, as a homage due to the merit of such a bright lover of music. With your approval, its success will be sure. I am, respectfully, and humbly your servant, monsieur F. J. Gossec.[2]

François Joseph Gossec

Saint-Georges concentrated on violin and composition until the winter of 1772-1773, when he played as violin soloist, at the Concert des Amateurs, two concertos for a principal violin with orchestra. These two concertos were his first compositions and in course of time acquired a decided vogue. Le Mercure, a Parisian periodical, wrote of Saint-Georges' first musical fruits:

> These concertos were played last winter at the Concert of Amateurs by the author himself and were received with the greatest applause as much for the merit of execution of playing, as for that of the composition.[3]

Later in June of the same year, Saint-Georges published six original string quartets by the music publisher Sieber. This establishes the fact that Gossec and Saint-Georges were the first French musicians who wrote string quartets. This type of composition, which was largely cultivated in Paris after the beginning of 1765, numbered among its representatives: Toeschi (1765), Hayden (1768), Gossec (1770), Jean-Chrétien Bach (1772) and now by 1773, Saint-Georges. The press, especially Le Mercure loudly reclaimed these works. That Saint-Georges' first compositions were so well received added to his fame as a fencer and established him as a serious musician and composer.

Gossec, who at this time was the conductor of the Concert des Amateurs was asked to preside over the Concert Spirituel along with Gaviniès, the violinist who was also, as I mentioned, a former pupil of Leclair, and Simon Le Duc.

Gossec resigned from the Concert des Amateurs and his pupil Saint-Georges inherited the conductor's position.

The Concert des Amateurs was founded through the determination of Gossec. The Concert Spirituel which was established already and had as its patrons the most distinguished persons. Gossec had produced some of his early works there with great dissatisfaction. The orchestra had remained the same for a long time with a small number of instruments, not enough, Gossec felt to present great pieces. Gossec approached the directors of the Concert Spirituel to try to convince them to gather together musicians and distinguished instrumentalists capable of performing symphonies in a large orchestra. Because of perpetual financial difficulties, the directors turned a deaf ear. Gossec was not discouraged. With the success of his comic opera, Les Pêcheurs, towards the end of 1766, he was appointed Intendant of Music to the Prince of Condé. With this powerful backer, he was able to convince two wealthy music lovers to found the Concert of Amateurs which quickly became, the best and the most celebrated in Europe. It was located at the Soubise Hotel. Despite what its name might imply, it was not an orchestra of amateurs. On the contrary, it was a great orchestra, the kind he was trying to put together for the Concert Spirituel.

The Concert of Amateurs did not please the privileged class who enjoyed the Concert Spirituel and did not welcome this rival. Difficulties arose. It was announced that no one would be admitted to the concerts of the Concert of Amateurs except shareholders.

Gossec was the director, and to make the orchestra even better, he placed Le Chevalier de Saint-Georges at the head of the orchestra. Saint-Georges was also one of the principal dancers. Saint-Georges ignited the orchestra. It had been a happy decision.

The rivalry broadened between the <u>Concert of Amateurs</u> and the <u>Concert Spirituel</u>. The <u>Concert of Amateurs,</u> supported by all the young and intelligent, easily crushed its adversary.

The orchestra of the <u>Concert of Amateurs</u> was a formidable one with 40 violins, 12 cello, 8 contrabasses, flutes, oboes, clarinets, trumpets and bassoons played by the most skillful artists of Paris. Gossec composed his great symphonies for this great orchestra. Gossec, through his direction made the Concert of Amateurs surpass the <u>Concert Spirituel</u>.

Ex. 18.1 Saint-Georges, Concerto, Op. V, No. 2, *Allegro moderato*

Page from Concerto Op. V No 2

Later, when the <u>Concert Spirituel</u> had almost fallen into disuse, he left the <u>Concert of Amateurs</u> entirely to Saint-Georges and he, Le Duc and Gaviniès as, I previously stated, went to take charge of the <u>Concert Spirituel</u> and to rebuild it. They succeeded. Once again the <u>Concert Spirituel</u> rivaled the <u>Concert of Amateurs</u>.

Saint-Georges conducted with great authority and was well respected by these great musicians. Although he conducted, he also on occasion played first violin.

The musical season had ten meetings and the quality of the music was widely praised. As well as conducting and playing, Saint-Georges composed several works. Two years after his first composition and his assuming the directorship, in June, 1775 he published a whole series of concertos for violin, opuses II, III, IV, and V.

> The gifted mulatto was then in the heyday of his creative activity and by the end of the year 1775, he had already written a collection of Symphonies concertantes, one of which was played on Christmas Day, at the Concert Spirituel.

Saint-Georges' standing as a musician was so firmly established that in 1776, he was considered for the post of assistant director at the Opera. The Royal Academy of Music as it was known, was at that time under the supervision of the city of Paris. Saint-Georges formed a company of capitalists and sought to put the organization under private supervision. He, of course, would be considered for the post of director or assistant director. According to Baron von Grimm in his Correspondance littéraire, philosophique et critique:

> This caused a great protest from Mesmoiselles Arnould, the opera singer, Guimard, the exceptional dancer, Levasseur, Rosalie, and other actresses, who signed a petition to the queen in order to represent to her majesty that their 'honor and privileges would not permit them to take orders form a mulatto'. Saint-Georges' request was rejected. Their honor indeed! Rubeluis said that when one thinks that Mesmoiselles Rosalie, Arnould and Guinard, these three divinities of the Opera were also famous for their licentious lives and their corrupt souls. It is suggested by some that the irritation of this rejection had contributed to rendering the mulatto more to the ideas of the Revolution that began to slowly spring up. On the contrary, Saint-Georges was a democrat at heart though reared as an aristocrat. A man of color, he had been born among the common people, and in sympathy, he remained one of them.[4]

> He went on to say: ...a young American known as the Chevalier de St.-Georges, combines the most gentle manners with incredible skill in all physical exercises and very great musical talent...but the artists nevertheless at once addressed a petition to the Queen.....

This kind of racist behavior must have hurt Saint-Georges very much but there was no appeal and apparently no attempts at revenge. He was talented and very successful. He simply moved on. Often, when people are pioneers, whether they realize it or not, they make the path easier for those who follow. St.-Georges was not trying to be a pioneer, he was only following his talents wherever they led. By being accepted by so many, it was easy for him to forget that he was a mulatto.

Alexandre Dumas, whose father served under St.-Georges at the beginning of the French Revolution probably benefited from the path that St.-Georges paved. He was born just two years after the death of St.-Georges. He never considered himself a black man; there is no evidence that he encountered overt racism during his life. He did, however, write a short work in 1843, entitled "Georges," in which he examined the question of race and colonialism. The main character was a mulatto who leaves Maritius to be educated in France and returns to his birth place to avenge his treatment as a boy. This, of course is the similar theme of <u>The Count of Monte Cristo</u>.

Saint-Georges continued his direction of the <u>Concert of Amateurs</u> successfully, although disappointed with the last venue. Even though his feelings had been damaged, he remained a very sensitive person. Shortly after, at the rehearsal of a symphony by the then deceased Le Duc, his great friend, which was to be played the following day at the <u>Concert of Amateurs</u>, Saint-Georges, in the middle of the adagio, "moved by the expressive quality of the composition, and remembering that his friend was no more, dropped his bow and burst into tears; his emotion communicated itself to all the artists, and the rehearsal had to be adjourned."

Saint-Georges was also interested in the theatre. In July, 1777, he presented a comedy in three acts with ariettes entitled Ernestine, at the Comédie italienne, which was the most frequented of the lyrical theaters. The words were by Choderlos de Laclos, author of Les Liaisons Dangereuses. The music was considered excellent, but its wretched libretto was responsible for its failure. Ernestine lasted only one presentation. "People even qualified it as a 'masterpiece of poor taste."

The Mecure admitted that the composer showed good qualities of style, much knowledge, as well as "facility and talent." The score has not been preserved, but a few fragments of its music are preserved in a collection of Saint-Georges' melodies, in the library of the Paris Conservatory. The subject of Ernestine was borrowed from a novel by Madame Riccoboni. Later, after having performed a second series of quartets, on October 12, 1778, he presented a new comedy with ariettes, <u>La Chasse</u> (The Hunt) at the <u>Comédie italienne,</u> which drew good size audiences. This time, the words were by M. Desfontaines, the author of <u>l'Aveugle de Palmyre and la Cinquantaine</u> and, of course, the music by Saint-Georges. Bachaument mentions the vaudeville air with which the piece concludes and prophesies that it will soon become popular. Friedrich von Grimm wrote of the music of <u>La Chasse</u> that:

The music of this drama is rather analogous to a poem. The public found in the composition of the musician, as in those of the poet, gaiety, agreeable details, happy passages; but there is also found dullness, common things and above all a great number of imitations and of reminiscences.[5]

Around this time, towards 1779, Madame de Montesson, the second wife of the Duke of Orléans, cousin of King Louis XVI, became very interested in Saint-Georges and his various talents in music. She was an occasional actress and writer, with a theatre at her house where plays and concerts were frequently given. Saint-Georges was appointed Superintendent of Music of her theatre. And an additional honor was paid him when she had Saint-Georges appointed and given the title of Lieutenant of the Hunt of Pinci. This appointment was an honor as well as a lucrative position. The additional money that this position brought was happily received by Saint-Georges who spent money freely and generously shared his good fortune with so many others.

Madame de Montesson circa 1780 after
Louise Élisabeth Vigée Le Brun (Versailles)

At the theatre of Madame de Montesson, Saint-Georges added acting to his talents as a conductor, composer, violinist and dancer. He conducted the concerts and directed plays in which he and Madame de Montesson occasionally appeared.

Saint-Georges' second position at the home of the Duke of Orléans and Mme de Montesson was far from a gratuitous one. Saint-Georges was an expert rider and one of the finest marksmen in France. It was said that once he set his eye on a target, he never failed to hit his mark. Hunting was one of the most popular of sports for the rich. In fact, King Louis XVI seemed to have loved hunting more than he loved being King but was not very good at either.

Rumors grew through the years that Saint-Georges' relationship with Mme de Montesson was much more than professional. Indeed, she was known to have admired him very much, but were they lovers? In his novel about Saint-Georges, Roger de Beauvoir goes into great detail regarding their alleged relationship. He describes her great love for him and her extreme jealousy [6]that eventually brought the relationship to an end. There is no proof of this alleged love affair, only artful rumors.

Saint-Georges was thus introduced into the social, artistic and political centers of the Royal Palace and became an intimate of the Duke of Orléans who became his friend and, as previously mentioned, his protector.

Also around 1779, Saint-Georges was chosen Musician with the <u>Concert Particuliers</u> of the Queen, Marie Antoinette, as second violinist.

Saint-Georges was very busy with his many duties and titles but he found time to continue composing, especially for the stage. In March, 1780, his <u>l'Amant anonyme</u> (The Anonymous Lover) was presented. In the second act, we discover one of those dialogue duets which delighted the music-lover of the day. The complete manuscript score is in the library of the Paris Conservatory. He composed <u>Le Droit du Seigneur</u> (The Right of the Lord). Little is recorded about this work.

Saint-Georges wrote romances which were very popular. They were sung everywhere, as far away as Brittany. A musical company of Rennes put several of them in their program. Their reputation went beyond the English channel to such an extent that "<u>L'autre jour ò l'ombrage</u> (The other day, in the shade of a tree), a romance sung by the delightful actress Louise Fusil during a meeting at the home of the Marquise de Champonas, has been conserved at the British Museum. Louise Fusil became one of St.-Georges' best friends.

Here is one of the stanzas whose words and music were composed by Saint-Georges.

> The other day in the shade of a tree
> A handsome young shepherd
> Sighed into the echo of the wood
> His plaintive song:
> Such troubles which accompany
> The joy of being loved!
> You come so reluctantly
> and flee so quickly!
> Love, let me die:
> My mistress has forgotten me:
> Life is such a torment
> When we are no longer loved.

Saint-Georges, still continuing with his unbelievable schedule, conducted at the Concert of Amateurs, and at the theatre of Mme de Montesson, played violin at the Royal Palace for the Queen, Marie Antoinette, performed his duties as the Lieutenant of the Hunt of Pinci and composed. Another not well known play was written by Saint-Georges entitled Les Amours et la mort du pauvre oiseau (The loves and death of the poor bird). There is no record of exactly when it was written or whether or not it was presented.

Around 1784, he resigned his position as the Superintendent of Music of the Duke of Orléans for unknown reasons and accepted the position of Director of Concerts of the Marquise de Montalembert, maintaining his other position and title of Lieutenant of the Hunt of Pinci. He was in charge at Mme de Montalembert's salon of regulating the musical part and performed certain roles in the plays. The wife of Général Marc René de Montalembert, La Marquise de Montalembert, had one of the best-known salons of that time. Not only the aristocracy was received at her house but good people of other classes as well. To be deemed "homme de beau temp", one had to be received at her house.

Again, as with other hostesses, Saint-Georges was rumored to have been romantically involved with Madame de Montalembert. It was even said that a baby was born from this affair and that the baby died or a white baby was substituted for it. These rumors allegedly came from a former lawyer of the parliament of Paris, Lefebvre de Beauvray, published in the salon of the Parisian Bourgeoisie. This is the same person who is thought to have been the architect of the attack on Saint-Georges and his friend by the policemen in disguise, which I described earlier.

This former lawyer lived not far from the hotel of the Marquise de Montalembert in the faubourg Saint Antoine, rue Popincourt. In the diary he dictated after he became blind, he then had it read by the friends who visited him. He dedicated two passages to Madame de Montesson. Here is what Lefebvre de Beauvray wrote:

> One speaks of the gallant intrigues of Mme de La Marquise de Montalembert who still lives with Le Marquis, her husband, rue de la Roquette. According to slander, this young lady was carrying on an affair with the

famous virtuoso, M. de Saint-Georges, a rich American Creole. It is even said that a child was born of this illegitimate relationship, but this child died (according to the rumor) sometime after birth. It is said that he could have been cured of the illness which carried him away but he did not receive the necessary care. Perhaps the punitive father, the husband of the lady, took advantage of the circumstances to get rid of a son which he had reason to believe was not his, without fanfare.[7]

Later Lefebvre de Beauvray wrote:

One no longer sees the sire Saint-Georges on rue de la Roquette. On what strange or foreign theatre has he gone to play the comedy which he no longer plays in public nor in private with Mme la Marquise de Montalembert on the theatre of her strange husband in the hotel occupied here in front of us by Monsieur le comte de Réaumur.

This theatre gives noble presentations but M. le Marquis persists still in refusing to admit commoners and bourgeoisie.

Probably M. Lefebvre de Beauvray was envious of M. Saint-Georges. Whether or not his second-handed rumors or allegations were true, it is obvious that he wanted to do damage with his statements. And why should one doubt that he could have masterminded the assault on Saint-Georges, along with Roland and Pierre?

During Saint-Georges' musical development, he made many new friends in all parts of the theatre. I have already mentioned several who were his teachers, his patrons, and his comrades in the theatre. There was one very famous and exceptional singer, Pierre-Jean Garat, who had great respect for the talents of Saint-Georges. They developed a warm friendship.

Pierre-Jean Garat was a very gifted singer and developed his talent at a very young age. By the time he was in his early twenties, he was already well known and respected as a fine singer. He was the favorite singer of Marie Antoinette, to whom he gave lessons. He gained a great reputation in all the capitals of Europe, and retained his voice for a long period. He became the "first professor of singing" at the Paris Conservatoire and had many famous pupils.

In the biography Garat by Bernard Miall, a portion is dedicated to Saint-Georges. Miall speaks of Saint-Georges in this way:

> Another companion of Garat's at this date (around 1787) was the Chevalier Saint-Georges, the idol of half the young bloods of Paris. His father was M. de Boulogne, a wealthy Creole of Guadeloupe, a farmer-general; his

mother was a negress. He was, for
a mulatto, undeniably handsome;
his physique was superb, his
muscular strength prodigious; he
excelled in every physical sport
and as a fencer was supreme. But
his attainments were not merely
physical; he was, a remarkable
violinist, whose skill drew crowds
in the garden of the Palais-Royal,
when his friends could persuade
him to play there by the moonlight.
His education had been, for those
days, unusually complete; his
manners were perfect; he was in
short, a coffee-colored Crichton.

A perfect dancer, he rode
like a centaur; he was also an
unrivaled skater. In the first
place master of horse to Mme de
Montesson, he was at this time
captain of the guard to the Duc
de Chartes. It was not strange that
this huge, exquisite half-breed had
a veritable court of admirers: not
only of the opposite sex. The first
school of arms in Paris was that of
the famous La Boëssière; poet and
swordsman, he had taught many of
the best swords in Paris, including
the redoubtable Saint-Georges.
His school, says Thiébault, was the

rendezvous of the best fencers...
forming the escort, and, so to
speak, the court of the Chevalier
de Saint-Georges, a true King at-
arms, and the first man in the world
in all matters of agility, strength,
and skill.

You can imagine the effect
he produced on me, who yielded to
no one in the matter of admiration
and enthusiasm...The strongest
fencers in the world were all
ambitious to fence with him, not to
dispute his advantage, but only to
be able to say, 'I have fenced,' or 'I
fence, with Saint-Georges!'

Saint-Georges had retained
a very great deference for his former
master, the aged La Boëssière. As
soon as he had assumed his lesson:
a courtesy lesson, which only
lasted a minute or two, but which
was very curious to witness...I
still seem to see him and hear him
call out, in his brusque tone and
his great voice: 'That won't do,
my children...Begin that again,
children!...At the right moment...
that's good children, that's good!'
And you will understand how this
man fascinated us, electrified us.[8]

A word or two again, regarding Saint-Georges' looks, it was unanimous that he was handsome, even his face, although as you may recall, his face was considered ugly by a few. Even with Garat, there is the condescending, "He was, for a mulatto, undeniably handsome." No, Saint-Georges was never completely accepted! In fact, notice that every reference to Saint-Georges mentions him as a mulatto, never a Frenchman or the like. In the following pages are copies of several paintings of St.-Georges, the original one that he sat for and some other artists paintings from memory. You decide.

On August 18, 1787, Saint-Georges presented a two-act piece, prose and ariettes at the <u>Comédie Italienne</u>, which he called <u>La Fille garçon</u> (The Girl Boy). The music of <u>La Fille garçon</u> was received with great applause, if we may credit the <u>Journal de Paris</u>.

Grimm, as I mentioned, gave reviews of two earlier plays by Saint-Georges. Here, he gives a summary of the plot and a critique of Saint-Georges and his music which was not consistent with the views of other critics of the time. He also offers an interesting point of view that should shed more light on the ambivalent feelings of some of Saint-Georges' contemporaries. Grimm wrote:

> August 18 (1787) was given on the Théâtre-Italien, the first presentation of <u>La Fille garçon</u>, a comedy in two acts and in prose, mixed with ariettes. The words were by M. Demaillot, who worked with much success for our little theatre of the boulevard and of the Royal Palace. The music is

by M. de Saint-Georges, mulatto, more famous by his prodigious talent for fencing, and by the manner, very distinguished, that he plays the violin, and by the music of two comic operas, <u>Ernestine</u> and la <u>Chasse</u>, which did not survive past their first presentations.

The Marquise of Rosane, having had the misfortune of losing her husband and her eldest son in the war, and wishing to save her only remaining son from the same fate, contrived to have her son raised as a girl and gave him to Nicette, the daughter of one of the farmers, for a companion. These two children developed the most tender friendship for each other and this feeling, with age, became love. The indiscretion of a neighbor of Madame de Rosane, who knew the secret, caused the mother and father of Nicette to suspect the truth; these suspicions caused Nicette's parents to hurry the marriage of their daughter with Jean-Louis, the neighboring Miller. Nicette hardly loves him and refuses an engagement that would separate her from her young friend. However, the young

Nicette addresses herself to the
same Jean-Louis in order to know
if he (her friend) is a boy or a girl,
as well as to make him suspicious
of everything that he felt for some
time; the responses of his rival left
him uncertain; he (the boy girl)
speaks finally to his mother who
no longer believes that she can
hide the truth. Her son, peaked
with joy, then asks her for the hand
of Nicette. The marquise tells him
how much the public voice would
blame a similar misalliance, but the
young man attempts to overcome
the resistance of his mother who
fears seeing him take part in the
army. He left her to reappear again
soon, redressed in the uniform
of dragon that this brother wore,
and announces to her at the same
time that he is going to go into the
service if she persists in refusing
him the hand of Nicette. This
threat causes Mme de Rosane who
consents to the union of the two
lovers.

Such is the end of this play
that the author, with the aid of
several useless scenes, delayed
for two acts. Just as the music,
although better written than any

other composition of M. de Saint-Georges, it appeared equally devoid of invention; the diverse pieces which compose it resemble, and by the themes, and even by the accompaniments, has some too well known pieces. This recalls an observation that nothing has yet refuted, it is that if nature has served the mulattoes in a particular way, by giving them a marvelous aptitude to exercise all the arts of imitation, it seems however to have refused them this zest of feeling and genius that alone produces new ideas and original conceptions. Perhaps also this reproach that I make to nature only involves a small number of men of this race to whom circumstances permitted to apply to the study of arts.[9]

It was racist then and still is today to suggest that ones color or racial ancestry determines ones ability to be creative. One can see all too clearly that Saint-Georges was sometimes disliked because of his color. M. Grimm's critique could have been one mans opinion had he not tried to be an anthropologist.

I have used many quotes about St.-Georges and his music to help to tell the story of this great man through the eyes of his contemporaries. So many flattering comments were made by so many people that I want you, the reader, to hear about how talented he was and what a wonderful human being he was. It must have been frustrating to be the most talented man around and still have some people who did not accept him. This behavior is the nature of the human being, regardless of race. It exists today and always will. St-Georges endured and prevailed.

In 1788, at the Théâtre des Beaujolais, Saint-Georges presented another comedy with ariettes, titled, <u>Le Marchand de Marrons</u> (The Seller of Chestnuts) and, in 1790, <u>Guillaume tout Coeur</u>.

Thus Saint-Georges' career as a composer ended in 1790. Paris was beginning a great change, indeed all of France was beginning to undergo a revolution that was to last for many years, changing the lives of every Frenchman.

To make clearer Saint-Georges' condition at this time, one must note that the Duke of Orléans died in 1785 and Saint-Georges lost his position as Lieutenant of the Hunt of Pinci. This loss enormously affected Saint-Georges' financial situation, for the position paid well. Remember, Saint-Georges lived well and spent generously.

André Grétry, a famous composer of comic opera, a contemporary and an admirer of the music of Saint-Georges, praised his music in his <u>Mémoires on Music</u>. He commented on one of Saint-Georges' symphonies and said of this particular piece:

> This last refrain has been employed in a symphony by the skillful artist Saint-Georges; it is repeated twenty times, and at the end of the piece, one is sorry to no longer hear it.

He went on to relate that:

> One night, walking in Thevenat Street, I sat on a street corner to hear this piece that was being played by a full orchestra in a neighboring house: it gave me a pleasure that has not been forgotten.[10]

This piece was by Saint-Georges.

Saint-Georges left numerous compositions for violin which make it possible for us to appreciate the adaptability and the varied nature of his talent as a composer, while at the same time testifying to his notable gifts as a violinist. He is known to have written: six Quartets for two violins, alto and bass, Op. I (1773); ten Concertos for a principal violin, violins I and II, alto, bass, oboe, flutes and two horns, comprising Op. II, III, IV, V, VII and VIII, which appeared from 1775 on; Symphonies concertantes for two principal violins; further, three Sonatas for the clavicorn or forte piano, with accompaniment of an obligato violin (1781); and finally, a posthumous work, preserved in the British Museum, consisting of Three Sonatas for violin, BIC.I (toward 1801), and of course, his romances and comic operas already mentioned.

> Saint-Georges' quartets are written in a clear, flowing ethereal style. More supple, more singing than that of Gossec, his melodies, notably in the rondos, well characterize the

sentimental and melancholic mulatto. Saint-Georges was at his best in his Rondeaux, and his little vaudevillian airs had given him a genuine reputation; all are instilled with movement, with grace, and are remembered with ease. We should recall that Haydn, too, chose flexible, lively themes for his finales. It is one of the musical pleasures of the epoch to rediscover symmetric divisions, to repeat incidental melodic phrases. The rounding-out, the return of the phrase in music, declares Grétry; '... makes up nearly its whole charm: In all Saint-Georges' works, the theatrical material shows grace, with a touch of Creole languor. The musician likes to repeat his themes, the second time in the lower octave. Very often, especially in the Rondeaux, they present repetitions of notes which give them a decided spruce ness and elegance.

A dashing and brilliant violin player, Saint-Georges was well aware of the effects to be drawn from motives in larger intervals, which his bow could slash out in bravura fashion. Like most musicians of his day, he showed a strong predilection for the multiple chromatic modulations which give the melodic movement a languorous and velvety touch.

As a technician of the violin Saint-Georges may be numbered among the most brilliant French virtuosi. Not only does he audaciously strive to reach the utmost limits of finger manipulation: he attains them; and in addition his bowing is vigorous and exact. He often plays chord passages at a rapid tempo; he dashingly sweeps up a ladder of skilled treble notes to drop brusquely back upon a deep sonorous tone. Or he carries out his broken-chord effects in the highest positions; in octaves and even in tenths. The suppleness of his bowing permits him to play variegated passages with the most fastidious perfection, and he handles double-stops like a master. He was at once extremely daring and skillful in passages demanding brio and brilliancy, and full of sentiment in the slow movements and Romances to which he was especially devoted. Together with

Gaviniès, Le Duc, Bertheaume and Paisible, the Chevalier de Saint-Georges worthy represents the French violin school of the second half of the eighteenth century.[11]

Saint-Georges was such a great violinist that a story is told that one night, he played a piece of music with his whip, a fact certified by witnesses. The whip in question became legendary; the handle was decorated by an infinity of precious stones and the Chevalier said that every one of those stars of his dazzling collection represented a woman who had loved him.

In 1786, the poet Moline had inscribed below the portrait of Saint-Georges, the following lines:

> Offspring of taste and genius, he
> Was one of the sacred valley bore,
> Of Terpsichore nursling and competitor;
> And rival of the god of harmony,
> Had he to music added poetry,
> Apollo's self He'd been mistaken for.

After the death of the Duke of Orléans in 1785, Saint-Georges needed to replace the loss of income that he had suffered with the Duke's death, thus he decided to go to London to engage in a series of fencing bouts with the most famous English and international fencing-masters. He arrived in England in the spring of 1787, taking a short leave from his musical enterprises.

Palais de Soubise

---

[1]Pincherele, Marc: Jean-Marie LeClair, L'ainé p. 117 Paris n.d.

[2]Gossec, F.J. d'Anvers: Paris 1766 n.p.

[3]Le Mercure de France, Avril, 1772 pp. 202-203

[4]Grimm, Diderot, Raynal, Meister et autres: Correspondence littéraire, philosophique et critique, Vols. 11, 12, 15

[5]Ibid.

[6]Beauvoir, Roger de

[7]Le Mercure de France, Août 1785

[8]Miall, Bernard: <u>Pierre Garat, Singer and Exquisite, His Life and his World</u>, 1762-1823 London 1913 pp. 95-97

[9]Grimm, Diderot, Raynal, Meister et Autres:

[10]Grétry: Mémoires ou Essai sur la Musique, Paris n.d. pp. 74-75

[11]Ibid.

Chapter IV

Saint-Georges in London

In England, his reputation as a fencer and musician was well known, and with the additional help of some indispensable letters of introduction which were very important to the English, he was admitted to the English aristocracy.

In London, Saint-Georges gave many fencing exhibitions and even fenced with Fabian, a friend and a famous professor from Paris. But the most celebrated of his duels was on April 9, 1787 with the Chevalière d'Eon de Beaumont. Attending this celebrated event were such famous sword fighters as Nogee, Reda, Rolland, Goddard, de la Motte, one of Saint-Georges' best friends, the Prince of Wales, later George IV, King of England and Angelo junior, the son of the famous fencing master, Henry Angelo. Henry Angelo senior had been the teacher of Mademoiselle d'Eon.

The senior Angelo left two works describing the life and times in England in the eighteenth century. I have already quoted from these books, Angelo's Pic Nic or Table Talk, and

Reminiscences of Henry Angelo. Angelo, of Italian heritage, was now an English citizen. He knew Saint-Georges well and every other fencing-master of that time admired his skills with the foil.

La Chevalière d'Eon (1728-1810) was born Charles de Beaumont d'Eon, a man. Much talk and many jokes circulated about this woman who had lived an entire lifetime as a man, who had an outstanding military career, but in his fifties, decided to put on the clothes of a woman and live a different life, "in order to perform in women's clothing, new and precious services to the French monarchy." Thus this gentleman Knight became a lady Knight.

Several books were written about the extraordinary career of this person. What was certain was that he was a great diplomat and a great fencer. He was known and respected in all the courts in Europe. Rumor had it that he had been born a girl and that his parents, having grown tired of having girls, decided to make her a boy.

One of the books about him by M. de la Fortelle, a contemporary of d'Eon's, has as its title:

> The military, political and private life of the demoiselle Charles Geneviève-Louise-Auguste-Andrée-Timothee Eon or d'Eon de Beaumont, esquire, knight of the royal and military Order of Saint-Louis, a former captain of dragons and of army volunteers, aide de camp of the maréchal and compte de Broglie, doctor in civil law and in droit canon, lawyer

of the Parliament of Paris, royal
censor for history and belles-
lettres. Sent to Russia secretly
at first then publicly with the
Chevalier Douglas for the meeting
of this court with that of Versailles,
secretary of the Embassy of the
Marquis de l'Hospital, ambassador
extraordinary to plenipotentiary of
France for his Imperial Majesty of
all the Russians, secretary of the
Duke of Nivernais, Ambassador
and plenipotentiary of France
and England for the conclusion
of peace, resident minister of
this Court after the departure of
the Duke of Nivernais, finally
plenipotentiary minister of France
in the same Court, known until
1777 under the name of Chevalier
d'Eon.[1]

The title of the book gives a summary of the life of the
Chevalier d'Eon. I will refer to our challenger as she, since it
was a she who came to fence with Saint-Georges.

It seems that she had retired on a pension of 12,000 livres
and could not live very well on it. An additional five thousand
pounds sterling was paid by Louis XVI to extricate her out of
her difficulties. Since she needed money, it wasn't too difficult
to persuade her to challenge Saint-Georges, in spite of her lack
of confidence due to her advanced age. So, she was there for
the same reason as Saint-Georges, to improve her finances.

In her book, The Chevalier d'Eon by Marjorie Corny, a complete account of this celebrated event is given. Here is the account of what took place:

> Carlton House was ablaze of lights. In the great drawing room, hundreds of candles shed their soft radiance over a crowd of fashionable men and bejeweled women who were pressed, seated or standing, around a small roped-off enclosure in the middle of the floor. Presently the buzz of conversation was stilled, and those who were seated rose to their feet as a pleasant-faced, rather stout young man entered the room, bowing in friendly fashion to right and left. Evidently the evening that the company awaited was of some interest and importance since the Prince of Wales himself was present as spectator. The Prince took his place, and the interrupted flow of conversation took up its course again. Then, another interruption as a young man in knee breeches, lace-finished white cambric shirt, neatly powdered hair and with a sword tucked under his arm made his appearance. He saluted the Prince and the company with his blade, and then stood, left hand

on hip, right knee slightly bent,
sword held in right hand, point to
the floor, in the typical graceful
waiting attitude of the fencer.
'Saint-Georges!   Saint-Georges!'
the whisper went round the room.
The young man was aware of the
admiring interest his appearance
caused, but was able to meet it
with an indifferent air; for he was
well used to admiration, the first
swordsman of England, the well-
named young Saint-Georges. In
the eyes of the women in particular
he found favor, and indeed he
made a pleasing enough spectacle,
lounging there in unembarrassed
grace, with his handsome head and
his athletic young body in all the
supple strength of its twenty-eight
years. But where was his opponent?
Indeed, where was any opponent
worthy of the steel of this glowing
young namesake of England's
Saint? The audience began to look
impatiently towards the door. And
then his opponent appeared-- this
opponent who should have been a
very war-god, to dare to face the
fresh young manhood that awaited
the combat there under the lights.
Walking slowly, apparently with

difficulty, there appeared in front of him a little frail old lady in a rusty black satin gown and white lace bonnet. The only touches of color about the whole amazing little person were the vivid blue of two unfaded, arrogant eyes in the white, shriveled face, and the flame color of a bit of ribbon on the black dress, over the left breast. The crowd craned their necks, tittered and whispered, as the old dame saluted the Prince with a plain, unengraved sword, which yet gleamed like fire. 'The Chevalier! Mademoiselle d'Eon! La Chevalière!' ran the whispers, as the quaint figure turned and saluted with shining blade the handsome young figure on the other side of the cleared space. Saint-Georges flushed. It was not of his seeking, this grotesque affair, and it was far from being to his liking. The thing had been forced upon him. One could not run the risk of being suspected of fearing an old lady, could one? Especially as that old lady had some reputation as a swordsman in the past. Doubtless, in the days long before Saint-Georges was

born or even dreamed of, when
Mademoiselle la Chevalière had
been Monsieur le Chevalier d'Eon
de Beaumont, her skill with the
sword had been passable enough.
But now-- bent with rheumatism
and age, shrouded and encumbered
in flowing draperies, the thing
was ridiculous. Saint-Georges
was ruffled out of his usual calm,
indignant at having been forced
to make a show of himself in this
fashion. He would not be hard
on the absurd old dame, but she
must be shown once for all, that
her ridiculous pretensions were
out of place and fashion. His
thoughts were cut short by the
sharp command of the official
who was to supervise the match;
'On guard, Gentlemen!' There was
some tittering at the 'Gentlemen,'
quickly stifled by a sharp glance
from the Prince. With an elegant
flourish of his weapon, Saint-
Georges put himself gracefully
on guard, and waited courteously
for his opponent. The odd person
in black satin assumed the same
pose, but with some considerable
difficulty. Indeed, a young lady
confided to a gallant, behind her

fan, she had distinctly heard the poor old thing's knees crack. The point of the shining, plain blade in its old-fashioned mounting quivered perceptively as it came forward to meet its opponent. Then, 'Go, Gentlemen!' and the two blades spoke sharply, each on its own tongue, as they made their first contact. Saint-Georges played negligently, lunging half-heartedly, contenting himself mostly with parrying; indeed, he scarce had need to parry, even; one step back and he was out of reach, those decrepit old legs could never furnish a lunge long enough to carry an attack home. Although really the old lady was stronger than one could have imagined, and her hand seemed now to be as firm as his own. Then an amazing thing happened. The old lady made an attack to the flank, and Saint-Georges lowered his hand to parry in octave. To his utter astonishment, no steel met his own, and in the same second he felt a sharp little blow on the upper arm, left unprotected by his lowered guard. There was no doubt about it. There was his opponent's blade

bent into an arc by the vigor of
the blow. He was astounded. The
trick was simple enough, but had
been executed with such a flashing
rapidity that he literally had not
seen the disengagement. But then
in truth, he had scarcely been
watching. 'Touché!' he announced
loyally. 'How generous! How
chivalrous!' murmured the ladies;
but some of the men raised their
eyebrows.

The adversaries put
themselves on guard again, and
again the 'Go, Gentlemen!' rang
out. Saint-Georges was watching
with all his eyes now. The old girl
had had a bit of luck, but she would
have to be contented with that. And
then suddenly he felt that horrible,
sharp little blow again; this time
in the side. This would never do.
He began to fight in earnest now,
using every trick he knew, making
the utmost of his superiority of
reach, and the unhampered stretch
of his legs. But again and yet again
he felt the irritating taps, light but
firm, as an attack reached home.
That relentless little old woman
before him seemed to have turned
into a veritable devil of strength

and agility, all steel nerves and iron muscles. Of the wrinkled, wasted face he saw only the fierce blue eyes. Of the ridiculous, almost crippled body he was aware only of a wrist and a hit like a steel spring. The shining blade, its deadly point safely buttoned, sang dizzyingly about his ears. He could neither find it with his own steel nor escape its wasp-like attack. Once a gasp of horror went up as the darting blade suddenly seemed to lengthen itself like a flame, hovered an instant a bare hair's breath before his unprotected eyes; the terrible 'coup de Nevers,' the death-dealing stroke between the eyes. At the last fraction of a second the steel spared his face, lowered and came home on his heart. A roar of applause greeted this tour de force, and cries of 'Bravo! Bravo, Mademoiselle d'Eon!' ran from the audience. The Prince himself was flushed with excitement and clapping vigorously.

Five times, six times, Saint-Georges' astonished lips announced a touch before the Chevalier's own voice rang out, 'Touché, Monsieur, and well done!' At Saint-Georges' eighth announcement, the bout came to an end amid a perfect storm of applause. Saint-Georges bit his lip. He was overwhelmed to accept so unexpected and crushing a defeat with any measure of philosophy. Then a wave of generous admiration welled up in him, and shouldering his way through the crowd that surrounded the victor, he bent and kissed the wrinkled old hand that was all a-tremble again now, and 'My respectful admiration, Madam,' he said. D'Eon pressed the young man's hand. 'Come and see me sometime Monsieur; I will show you a trick or two. You have the makings of a very gallant swordsman.'[2]

There is no doubt that this duel took place on the given date but to this particular account, there is great doubt as to the details, as they are presented by the author. The most obvious error is that she states that Saint-Georges was 28 years old. According to his date of birth, he was 48 years old, or even if one takes the other date given in memoirs of several of his contemporaries as his birth date, that of 1748, he would have been 39.

It seems that this author wished to present her heroine in the most favorable light, and it seems at the expense of Saint-Georges' reputation as a fencer. I do not wish to be accused of doing the same for the hero of my book, but I cannot accept this account which is contrary to everything that has been written about Saint-Georges.

I have given reports of Saint-Georges' prowess as a fencer from La Boëssière, one of the greatest fencing-masters of the time, and from other duels that he had with such notables as Faldoni, one of the best fencers of that time. It was said that Saint-Georges was "inimitable and invincible" and from all the sources, there was no match for Saint-Georges. Now, this account assumes to reveal that Saint-Georges was not only beaten but completely out-classed and did not even touch this "little frail old lady, walking slowly, apparently with difficulty."

I fear that I may seem less objective but it is difficult for me to believe that an old lady in her sixties, "But now-bent with rheumatism and age, shrouded and encumbered in flowing draperies," could do what younger, and supposedly greater, fencers could not do. The author makes Saint-Georges look even worse by saying that:

> The odd person in black satin assumed the same pose, but with some considerable difficulty. Indeed, a young lady confided to a gallant, behind her fan, she had distinctly heard the poor old thing's knees crack.

She also describes La Chevalière in this way.

> Of the wrinkled, wasted face he saw only the fierce blue eyes. Of the ridiculous, almost crippled body he was aware only…

Other people who were present at this historical event gave varying reports on the duel. And according to one of these reliable reports, Saint-Georges had been touched twice by Mme d'Eon, that Saint-Georges "unfolded, unraveled, rapid as the wind, and he also struck her."

> The roar that he made had made the Prince laugh; the strike also; right in the middle of her chest or breast since we are speaking of Chevalière. Some feared that there would be a second offense, which would have been a little to the right, or a little to the left…but the chevalier was too gallant a man to commit this fault of good taste. The English would have, in the name of propriety, misunderstood that.[3]

However, Mme d'Eon was awarded the victory.

Robineau, a French artist, executed a painting on this subject, from which a print was published. According to the account given by Marjorie Corny, the elder Angelo was not present and was told of the news later, yet according to the Obituary Notice of the Chevalier D'Eon in "Gent. Mag." June 1810, Angelo was there. This inference supported out in a statement about the painting by Robineau:

> The celebrated painter alluded to by the writer was doubtless Robineau, whose picture is the subject of the accompanying

illustration. The figure to the left
of the Prince's chair observing
the match through a spyglass is
probably intended for the elder
Angelo. Henry Angelo was one of
the Chevalier's antagonists on this
memorable occasion.[4]

And from the Chevalier d'Eon de Beaumont by J. B.
Telfer, it is stated that Angelo, Senior was present

...we almost lost sight of
her (d'Eon) until April 9, 1787, the
day appointed for an assault-at-
arms in the presence of the Prince
of Wales at Carlton House, and to
which, as a fencer of distinguished
reputation, she was invited. D'Eon
and M. Angelo, Senior were
nominated by his Royal Highness
judges for the occasion...[5]

Also, from the same book, there is word about the duel.

Mademoiselle d'Eon had
modesty enough, on her hitting
Monsieur de Saint-Georges, to
set it down to his complaisance;
but the latter candidly declared
that he had done all in his power
to ward against it." Angelo's son
wrote regarding the portrait that:

"I was one of the exhibitors on that day; my father's portrait is in the background."

Finally, Saint-Georges was a gentleman who was known not to have ever taken advantage of anyone. His gentleness and kindness were as well known as his fencing.

Saint George D'Eon Robineau

This "defeat" did not tarnish Saint-Georges' image, it only helped to spread his fame. He was well received in the most aristocratic salons; the people considered him "the most seductive of colored gentlemen." The Prince of Wales was so enthusiastic about Saint-Georges that he wanted to decorate him with the "Ordre du Bain," (Order of the Bath) but Saint-Georges had the modesty to refuse it.

Saint-Georges was received by the English ladies as enthusiastically and as affectionately as he had been by the women in Paris. Indeed the women were not cold, as people had said; a little prudish, maybe, but certainly not cold. He found that he was accepted, it seemed with a certain peculiarity, as a gentleman but there was no prejudice shown. But why should he be surprised? Didn't he find the same behavior in his beloved Paris?

This brings to mind an incident that occurred in Paris, regarding one of Saint-Georges' amorous adventures. Saint-Georges was the lover of a pretty woman. They were seen together all over Paris and the relationship became quite a big affair. People began talking of marriage although Saint-Georges had not considered it. One day, he was paid a visit by the brother of his sweetheart. The brother spoke to Saint-Georges very firmly saying,

> My sister has a weakness
> for you, I know that's between
> you two. But as concerns all of
> my family, there is a rumor going
> around about a marriage between
> you. Now, I tell you very clearly
> that is impossible. We would
> oppose this by all means and even
> by violence. I have spoken.[6]

It becomes easier to see just what Saint-Georges' position really was. The French people, like the English and other people who are prejudiced have their degrees of prejudice. One need only scratch deep enough, and, in this case, Saint-Georges had gone far enough. If this story were true, that would have been the second time that St.- Georges had faced the same threat and rejection. Being the greatest fencer in the world, he could have taken these threats as insults, therefore, an excuse for a dual. But St.- Georges showed time and again that he did not take advantage of his superior skill as a swordsman except in exhibitions, to defend his person and later during the war.

Odet Denys recounts or invents a curious occurrence between Saint-Georges and an English woman who did not seem at all to notice his color. They were in a little alcove and were exchanging intoxicating kisses, when she stopped and in a mournful cry, she said in English.

> It is not love, it is only passion; and then she continued in French saying 'non', but right away, with no transition, she squeezed him strongly against her, and, freed from the scruples the homage she had paid to purity, with all she let loose, abandoned herself in his arms in pronouncing these delirious words.[7]

Since St.-Georges was a ladies man, I am sure many such incidents occurred, but this one was most likely invented. Nothing this intimate has ever been documented, so I pass this on as an invented anecdote.

Saint-Georges was not only received by women, the men invited him to many parties and meetings. There were lavish parties and expensive dinners and such a gay life. Naturally,

Saint-Georges was very generous by nature and cared very little for amassing a large sum of money, only enough to live the good life that he lived. Said Angelo:

> ---but the various talents of Saint-Georges were like a mine of gold he might have amassed considerable wealth, if he had united prudence to his other qualities.He was very liberal in money matters and indulged freely in all the pleasures which then made Paris such a delightful residence.[8]

Thus Saint-Georges' trip might have been marvelous in one sense but he gained very little money. The truth is that the only money that Saint-Georges took back to Paris was 200 guineas that he won in a bet from the Prince of Wales that he could jump a very wide ditch in Richmond with his knees together, that is without taking a running start.

While Saint-Georges was in London, he had an incident similar to the one he experienced earlier in Paris. The story was told that he was walking at night when suddenly before him a thief threatened with a pistol. With a stick he brought the man to his feet. He did the same for three other bandits who had come to help their comrade. Although left with several contusions, he continued calmly on his way home, where he was awaited to play the violin and to entertain the invited guests.

Saint-Georges then left London with probably less money than he had brought. His sojourn had not been successful financially.

He took back to Paris the English fashions of frockcoat, round hat, and boots "that dethroned forever the embroidered clothes and short pants." Saint-Georges had been a fashion setter before coming to England. He used to walk down the boulevards after theatrical presentations and young people surrounded him, followed him, and courted him. He became a fashionable man. It had been said that Saint-Georges was the forerunner of the English Beau Brummell.

After one of Saint-Georges' fêtes, he wrote a letter that reveals again his generosity. He constantly gave expensive gifts, especially to men of arms and of music. Here is a copy of the letter that he wrote:

Letter of M. de Saint-Georges to M. Teillogori, on the subject of what happened at the reception of M. Etienne, last Wednesday, March 11

Paris, this 15th of March 1772

I am indisposed, Sir; otherwise I would have had the occasion to see you and compliment you and tell you what a pleasure you have afforded me and to all the experts at the reception of M. Etienne. You have shown that manly confidence that one sees only in superior men. And in all you have done, one could see the great marksman. If you had won the prize, merit and talent would have been rewarded, but you are above all that. I beseech you, Sir, in the name of all connoisseurs to accept the sword I send you. It will be glorious for one to have placed it in the hands of the sincere attachment with which I have the honor of being, Monsieur,

Your very humble servant, De Saint-George[9]

Saint-Georges returned to Paris the summer of 1787 and resumed his musical career. The fruits of that labor have already been recounted.

During Saint-Georges' most productive years musically, he was carrying many responsibilities as well as composing, he still found time to continue his social life. He frequented the salons and attended many parties. Now that he had added music to his well-established fame as a fencer and man-about-the-town, he was invited to more parties than he could attend.

I have not said very much about Saint-Georges' other well-known qualities, that of a conversationalist and as an excellent dancer. These great men of sports and theatre loved to make good conversation at the salons and at the dinners and parties. Saint-Georges was considered a man of good ideas and of intelligent and witty words. It was known that he was not only a man who excelled in corporal exercises and at the violin but also a man who had ideas and could express himself very well. He had an infectious laugh that was imitated by people around him. A party was successful and more enjoyable when he was present.

As a dancer, he excelled. Angelo junior told of a time having been entertained by him in Paris:

> ---returning to France, Chevalier pressed Mr. M'D---- _____ and myself to dine with him at La Sablonières'. After an excellent dinner, bien servi, in the evening he introduced some of the first dancers, Madame Saunier, etc., of the orchestra (with their instruments), Chabran, Sulpeatro, and Florio, selected by him purposely for our amusement. All was gaitié à la Française, la

danse et la musique, the toe and
the elbow keeping motion, whilst
the champagne and burgundy
enlivened the scene. We were both
well pleased with the politeness
and attention of the maître de
ballet.[10]

He was in demand as a dancer and attended balls several
times per week. He had a natural feeling for rhythm perhaps
from his island culture and his natural grace, combined with
excellent training. Since dancing was as much a part of French
life as wine and sports, Saint-Georges would travel miles at
great expense to be a part of these great balls. Unfortunately,
in his forties, Saint-Georges broke an Achilles tendon that
curtailed somewhat his dancing and even interfered with his
speed in fencing.

Towards the end of the year of 1789, Saint-Georges
returned to London accompanying the new Duke of Orléans, the
future Philippe-Égalité into exile. The Duke, while pretending
to have new reforms to introduce into the French fashion, was
actually engaging in politics. Saint-Georges was not aware of
the Duke's true purpose.

He was again received by His Royal Highness, the
Duke. While the Duke of Orléans went his way, Saint-Georges
was once again received in the aristocratic circles. It is not
exactly clear how long he stayed in London this time, but he
did stay much longer than before, since he had a well-furnished
apartment. Angelo Junior presents evidence of this apartment
in relating this story:

For some years, I had a fencing room at the Opera-House Haymarket, over the entrance of the pit door. On the evening of June 17, 1789, about eight o'clock, when in Berkeley-square, I saw a black smoke ascending; and soon hearing that there was a fire in the Haymarket, I directly hastened there, when to my surprise, I beheld the Opera-House in flames. Having the key of my room in my pocket, and the crowd making way for me, I soon got there, at the time the back part was burning. I first secured the portrait of Monsieur Saint-Georges (the famous fencer), which hung over the chimneypiece, and removed it to Saint Albin's street, where I then resided. At my return, though, I was not absent six minutes, the mob had rushed in, and plundered the room of everything. As to the foils, jackets, etc., they were of little value to me, compared to what I had in my closet: a portfolio of beautiful drawings, particularly several valuable ones of Cipriani, also of Nortimer, Rowlandson, etc., the loss of which I very much regretted; but consoled myself by saving Saint-Georges' picture, which he sat purposely for, and offered me after our fencing together, the second day of his arrival in this country. It was painted in 1787 by Mather Brown, an American artist, much encouraged here at the time.[11]

There exist a great number of drawings representing the Chevalier de Saint-Georges. First, there is the portrait in dark brown by Carle Vernet, and another portrait that hung in the arms room of Professor Grisier:

> ... the physiognomy, distinguished, stands out an enormous white tie. The Chevalier wears a scarlet frock, and his hand, covered by a big fencing glove, holds a foil.

This is one of the few remaining portraits and the one that appears most often in literature of Saint-Georges. This portrait is an aquatint made in London while Saint-Georges was staying in London. There exists another picture from the same period, colored, and showing la Chevalière d'Eon making an assault with the Chevalier. It has a title: The assault, on fencing match, which took place at Carlton House, on the 9th of April, 1787, between Mademoiselle la Chevalière d'Eon de Beaumont, and Monsieur de Saint-Georges.

In this picture, English as its title says, the famous Chevalière d'Eon, wearing a black dress, leaving the arm free for bending, wearing cornets ridiculous enough, and the cross of Saint-Louis on her chest, crosses swords with Saint-Georges, in leather jacket and in knee breeches. Among the spectators is the Prince of Wales. Other contemporary drawings, rarer, sketched mostly in crayon representing different strokes of dexterity of Saint-Georges. Here, he can be seen jumping through the half-opened doors of a coach riding speedily; farther, he kills with each hand several swallows in their flight. The most amusing of these drawing is the Duel à l'écumoire (The Duel with the Skimmer) sketch attributed to Carmontel. The Chevalier, in little morning jacket, and crossing swords against a cook of the Prince de Conti, who, tired of the reproaches of Saint-Georges about his cooking, had called him moricaud (darky) and had thrown himself on the mulatto, in the kitchen, sword in his hand. Obliged to defend himself and without arms, the Chevalier had grabbed

a skimmer and, with this peculiar
sword, disarmed his vindictive
adversary. Saint-Georges, who
held his title of Creole very highly,
did not in the meantime like to
be called 'darky' witnessed by
the miserable fellow that he rolls
in the gutter to make him pay for
this unwelcome expression, telling
him, 'there you are now, as dark as
I am.'[12]

It is fortunate that the English recorded many more
anecdotes about Saint-Georges and his accomplishments, but
not many about his social life. I chose to quote these adventures,
since they describe the events so vividly that I fear that some
of the charm and authenticity might be lost by my telling these
anecdotes in my own words. Since Saint-Georges' talents and
exploits will appear unbelievable to many, I chose to let the
people who knew him tell his story, even though sometimes
there is controversy regarding some events that led some to
interpret differently; nevertheless, they verify that the events
did occur.

Here again is another account of Saint-Georges told
again by Angelo junior, who saw him often while he was in
London:

Monsieur Chevalier, at that
time first dancer at the Opera house
here, and who was considered one
of the best fencers at Paris, was a
constant visitor, not only assisting

in improving my scholars, but gratifying me, for I ever preferred to be opposed to a scientific antagonist. Mr. M'D and Chevalier were usually opponents, and one day, the former being displeased at received the other's thrust, after having given the first hit, some words arose between them, which I did not hear, when they left off. They dressed themselves and quit the room together; finding that on the stairs they had some angry conversation (this was in June about three o'clock), and had both gone, I suspect some appointment had been made. As soon as I could get away, I hurried to the Orange coffeehouse to find out the Chevalier's address, where I found him in high spirits over a dish of macaroni, perhaps confident of his superior skill with a sword. Though I could not get the least information from him, as to whether any intended meeting was to take place, I was determined to watch his leaving the house. About five a hackney-coach stopped before the door, bringing Mr. M'D_____t and Monsieur Henry with him; soon after, Chevalier entered, when the coach drove towards Pimlico. I directly followed. After passing the turnpike, it turned to the left toward Pimlico, and stopped at the end of a lane, some little distance from Chelsea Hospital. Here, they descended. I was then some way off, running; however, I was in time to see them get over a gate, when hastening to the place, in a field, I saw them with their coats off, sword in hand, just going to engage; I called out, and ran towards them, but not in time to prevent them from beginning. Here was a commencement, far different to those methods they had previously practiced before me in the Haymarket, as caution and skill are necessary when opposed to the point of a sword. Fortunately the delay, caused by the hesitation who should attack first, enabled me to be in time to part them. When I inquired what could be their motive for going out with swords, or whether anything had been said to give offense, or any apology expected, they both seemed not to know what brought them at that distance together. All that I could elicit was, Chevalier was called out, and he said, 'de tout mon Coeur.' To give you an idea of the short time I beheld the grand combat, the Frenchman, endeavoring to intimidate his adversary, kept making a noise; though he made the first lunge, he took good care to be out of distance at the time, whilst the other, whom I had often seen not so cool and collected with a foil, now with all that sang froid, laughed, and cried, 'poh!' on his first receiving the attack, and at Chevalier's not coming nearer. This faire semblant of the one to appear courageous to frighten, or the other's fierté, could not have continued long; the result might have been dangerous, or fatal.

Now peace having been pro-claimed, and the swords sheathed, we all adjourned to a tea-garden, near Hogmorre Lane, where the glass passed round pretty freely. Chevalier, who at Paris had often drawn his sword, showed us sufficient proofs of the different rencontres he had experienced there, his right side and breast exhibiting many places where he had been wounded. As the wine operated, he began to boast of his amours, and told us that his mistress had once stabbed him, through jealousy, showing us a scar on his right breast, and though we considered it at the time as a mere histoire, yet we patiently listened to his adventure. After this last bout, unlike the classical opponents, they always met with good humor and found my room preferable to the field.[13]

Notice, finally, this peculiar detail that sums up the attitude and respect the English had for Saint-Georges as a man of arms:

...this retired fencer, this master of arms, who was called the inimitable and the invincible, never had a duel. No adversary dared risk a duel with him. In fact, his historic duel with a fencing master, the Chevalier de la Morlière is only a comedy. The story is known. Saint-Georges outraged, fixed an appointment with his adversary under one of the arches of the Mary Bridge and, there on his body broke a whole bushel of foils, to the great amusement of the dumbfounded onlookers. The

Chevalier de Saint-Georges is in every way one of the most original figures of his time.[14]

J.A. Rogers when writing of this same story, wrote that:

But the Count proved so poor an opponent, that Saint-Georges seized him boldly, put him across his knees and spanked him like a child....

"I shall conquer this"

Watercolor of Henry Angelo's Fencing Academy, by Rowlandson, 1787. Famous fencer, Chevalier St. George's portrait, foils, and fencing shoes are on the right wall.

[1]Fortelle, M. de la: La vie militaire, politique et Privée de demoiselle d'Eon, Paris 1811

[2]Corny, Marjorie: The Chevalière d'Eon. London 1932

[3]Unknown

[4]"Gent Mag." Obituary Notice of the Chevalière D'Eon, June 1810

[5]Telfer, J. Buchan: The Chevalière D'Eon De Beaumont, published 1885, Paris

[6]Unknown

[7]Denys, Odet, Qui était Le Chevalier de Saint-Georges, Paris 1972

[8]Angelo, Henry The Reminiscences of Henry Angelo, Vol. II Paris 1830

[9]National Archives of Paris 1789-1799

[10]Angelo, Henry…Reminiscences…Vol. II pp. 308, 309

[11]Angelo, Henry…Reminiscences…pp. 398, 421

[12]Larousse, Grand Dictionnaire Universel du 19e Siècle, Vol. XIV, Paris 1875, pp. 68, 69

[13]Angelo, Henry Angelo's Picnic or table talk, pp 21-25, London, John Ebers 1834

[14]Larousse, Grand Dictionnaire Universel du 19e Siècle, Vol. XIV, Paris

Chapter V

Return to Paris
The Beginning of the Revolution
Saint-Georges Serves His Country

After a lengthy stay in London, Saint-Georges ended his second and final visit and returned to Paris. He immediately resumed his stylish way of living and wrote a few more pieces of music which were published in London after his death.

Saint-Georges led a very unusual life even for those times. Maybe, because he was black, he had more than the usual encounters. Since he was such a great fencer and such a gentleman who was noted for never taking advantage of a person, it should seem odd that he would have so many duels and attacks. I have only mentioned a few specific instances of attacks on Saint-Georges, but there were many more attacks on him as he walked the streets at nights. Certainly some had nothing to do with his color, they were simply attempted robberies. Yet others cause one to question. Saint-Georges was such a kind and forgiving man. Denys tells us that:

> Once during a discussion with one of his rivals at the Concert of Amateurs, he had made a few unpleasant remarks to the other man and the other man slapped him. The injury was one of those which one considered provoking a fight and the invincible sword of Saint-Georges held this careless man at his mercy. But as Saint-Georges was as quick to catch himself as to loose himself, he contented himself with saying to the witness at the scene, 'I like his talents too much to fight him.' Only the reputation for goodness which the Chevalier enjoyed can explain the boldness of this violinist, for Jarnowick was not a good swordsman; he had sometime later in England insulted a pianist and obstinately refused to fight and lost face to the point that he had to leave London.[1]

In 1789, the French Revolution began. This period extended to 1799, beginning on May 4, 1789, with the meeting of the States-General which desired to suppress class distinctions and secure the system of voting by head. In effect there was a desire to destroy the system of Feudalism. France, like several other European countries, was a class society with definite inequality of rights. There were three orders of estates. Out of a population of 24 to 36 million people in the 18th century, 96 percent were of the Third Estate or the lower class people who paid almost all of the taxes. About 500,000 people made up the privileged classes divided between the ecclesiastical and aristocratic which were the first and second estates who paid almost no taxes.

French peasantry was unique in Europe in that all peasants were legally free and about 3 out of every 4 heads of families were proprietors of the land they worked. They owned about 40 percent of the workable land but with a growing rural population, it was not enough. Since their small plots were inadequate to support them, they had to earn extra money by working the land of the clergy, the aristocracy or the bourgeoisie as tenant farmers or sharecroppers. One out of every 4 was landless. These families had to hire themselves out as farmers, etc. Because of this group, France had thousands of beggars, tramps and robbers, even during good times. This group was also almost entirely illiterate.

Under this feudal system, the peasants were not allowed to shoot game on the land owned by the seigneurs (nobles or bourgeois, or a prosperous peasant). Even when the pigeons or rabbits were feeding on the land of the peasant's crops, they were forbidden by law to shoot them. The peasants had to pay to use the mills, bake-houses, etc., of the seigneurs. They had to pay tolls on roads and bridges; and there were many other dues. The peasant could not win in court, because most of the judges were landowners.

The administration of civil justice was weak. Many of the law officers were staggeringly incompetent and corrupt. Legal principles concerning persons and property varied from area to area. In all the myriad courts which covered the country, procedure was slow and costly. Often it was cumbersome, frequently dishonest. As for the barbarous procedure of criminal justice, it was shocking to the humanitarian consciousness of the age. The taxation system, too, was the product of historical growth and reflected social and economic evolution. The most crushing direct taxes were levied on the peasantry, while the upper classes enjoyed partial or total exemption. There were also burdensome indirect taxes which were given out under contract for collection. Of these, the gabelle, or the tax on the sale of salt, which was a government monopoly, was the most onerous, unjust and hated. There were outrageous variations in price, which ranged from thirteen sous a pound in many regions to only one sou elsewhere, and there were the sharpest differences in the amount that householders were compelled by law to buy per annum. In consequence, smuggling was rampant, and between the smugglers and the government, there was an undeclared war. No other aspect of the Old Regime was so cleverly criticized as the fiscal system, but it remained unchanged to the end.

Like any revolution, the French Revolution did not happen in a day or a week, it was long in coming; it was inevitable. Many great changes were needed. But the French Revolution, unlike other revolutions, was not born of a conspiracy. Forces were in action to bring about change but no one envisioned that the results would be a revolution.

Since Louis XIV, France had spent a great deal of money in many wars. Louis XV and Louis XVI were both weak and inept as rulers. For many years, about 75 percent of the French budget went for the military. Moreover, the decision to back the American Revolution cost France dearly. From 1766 on, French ministers of Finance tried to raise money, but were not successful. Between great opposition from the Parliaments of Paris, the Third Estate and a weak, unresponsive king, who spent much of his time hunting, France was headed for drastic changes.

The French system broke down mainly because of three crises in the areas of politics, finances, and the economy.

The most immediate problems of the people were land shortage and the high price of bread. This reminds me of the now famous story of the people addressing the Court in regards to this problem with Marie Antoinette responding with her now famous statement, "Let them eat cake." There were bread riots in the spring and early summer of 1789. Abbeys and manor-houses were attacked and no longer were the laws against killing game respected. Game was killed and trapped illegally. The peasants ceased to pay dues.

On June 17, 1789, the Third Estate broke away from the First and Second Estates and formed a new group, called the National Assembly. Eventually, the First and Second Estates joined them in order to find a fair way to raise taxes.

In the same month, Louis gathered troops outside of Paris. The people feared that he was going to try to take power from the assembly. So, on July 14, 1789 they stormed the Bastille, set the few prisoners loose and tore down the prison. This was the beginning of the French Revolution.

Saint-Georges was in sympathy with the Revolution although he was an aristocrat. He was a black man, and the cause of the underprivileged was his as well. He thought that the Revolution against the Old Regime could possibly effect changes in slavery in his island homes of Guadeloupe and San Domingo.

During all this turmoil, Saint-Georges continued performing his music. In 1791, he put together a group to perform some concerts. Among these musicians were his good friend Lamotte, the horn player, and the actress Louise Fusil. He gave concerts at Lille in 1791, where he stayed for a while. The documentary evidence of the archives informs us that Saint-Georges was living in Lille in 1791, and that for two years, he was a captain in the National Guard there.

After these concerts, Saint-Georges continued on to Tournai, which was Austrian at that time, to perform some concerts there. It has been stated that these concerts at Tournai were just excuses for his real purpose, which was political. The account goes on to say that Saint-Georges was pretending to organize a concert, when he was actually sent by the Duke of Orléans to speak with several émigrés to illicit their support for the Duke. Of course, this was false since the Duke had no ambitions of being king of France even though he had many supporters. St.-Georges was not given a friendly welcome. The people there thought him a man of inferior race who really represented the Duke. They refused to accept him at their table. Saint-Georges had to leave Tournai after an insult from the commander. According to Louise Fusil who was with his group, there was no hint of any political role played by Saint-Georges at the request of the Duke of Orléans. But the account of his short stay in Tournai goes on to say that:

> The commander of the place had forbidden Saint-Georges to be seen in public. At the hotel where he had gone, someone had the impertinence to turn down the plate which Saint-Georges had turned up to eat and Saint-Georges so superior in the art of

peculiar vengeance, had the good
spirit not to show any humor for
these actions, which he could
scarcely censure with injustice and
he hastened to return to France. It
was a good action on the part of a
man who excelled in the art of this
particular vengeance.

It is a matter of record that the incident occurred, but as
to his political purposes in Tournai, the rest is only conjecture.
Although the former Duke of Orléans was his friend and
protector, and Mme de Montesson had been his friend and
comrade in the theater at her house, Saint-Georges did not
feel obligated to be used by the Duke of Orléans. There is
no evidence that his mission was other than what he stated,
especially since, later, they chose separate paths politically.

Going back a short time to October 6, 1789, after the July
storming of the Bastille, there was a second attempt of a coup
d'état which led to the capture of the king and the royal family
at Versailles by a mob from Paris. The Royals were transferred
to Tuileries Palace in Paris. The king attempted to flee on June
20, 1791, but was arrested. He became a constitutional king,
taking his oath of office on September 13, 1791. The King,
then, plotted with Austria and Prussia to overthrow this new
government.

France declared war on Prussia and Austria in 1792
which began the French Revolutionary Wars. Saint-Georges
decided to come to the aid of his country.

In September, 1792, Saint- Georges asked the National
Assembly to allow him to form a corps of "colored" troops to
aid France in the war. There were, at that time, a number of

"freed Negroes," from the West Indies who had come to France to offer their services in the war.

The National assembly agreed to allow Saint-Georges this honor. So, St.-Georges recruited these brave souls and formed a group that was called the National Legion of Midi. He was given the rank of Colonel. He chose as his lieutenant colonel, Alexander Dumas, who was to become a distinguished General in the army of Napoleon and the father of one of France's greatest and most prodigious writers, Alexander Dumas, père.

The name of this group was later called the American Hussards. Sometimes Saint-Georges himself was referred to as an American, meaning from the area of America. The name of the regiment was changed to Legion of Men of Color. Sometimes it was called Saint-Georges' Legion. It finally became the 13th Regiment of Hunters, then the Horse Hunters.

Mounted trouper of Saint-Georges Legion

After their training period, the soldiers were sent to take part in the army in Belgium. The commander of that Army was General Charles François Dumouriez. General Dumouriez had already distinguished himself with his victory over the Prussians at Valmy on September 20, 1792. He handily defeated the Austrians at Jemappes on November 6.

Saint-Georges led his men into battle with enthusiasm and valor in several engagements. He distinguished himself by his sound decisions and by his bravery. But soon after, the tide turned and the Army of Dumouriez with Saint-Georges' troops were repulsed and twice defeated on March 18 and 21, 1793.

While Saint-Georges was pursuing his military career, the National Convention in Paris was going full speed with the Revolution. The National Convention formed in September and soon after, on September 21, 1792, the Convention declared royalty abolished. In January, it tried the king for his treason against the nation and condemned him to death. He was executed on January 21, 1793. The last member of the Convention was the Duke of Orléans, Saint-Georges' friend and cousin to the king. He voted to condemn the king, partly out of the fear that as a Bourbon, a member of the royal family, and already under suspicion, he might endanger himself more by voting against the condemnation. Also the Duke and the King had never liked each other anyway.

After the death of Louis XVI and of his queen, Marie Antoinette, all of France went through a period of disorder and violence. Anyone suspected of treason or hostility to the revolution was imprisoned or summarily beheaded. More than 18,000 men, women and children were sentenced to the guillotine. This lasted until 1799, when Napoleon Bonaparte took control of the government.

After the defeats of Saint-Georges' Legion, the Regiment returned to Lille to protect the city in case of attack. Towards March 30, 1793, the Convention decided that Dumouriez should be summoned to appear before their body. Four commissaries were sent to bring him in. Dumouriez arrested the commissaries and handed them over to the Austrians, and then attempted to persuade his troops to march on to Paris and overthrow the revolutionary government. He was now conspiring with the enemy. He had made certain promises to the Austrian Colonel Mack, Chef d'Etat-Major of the Prince of Coboury. Deserting with Dumouriez was the son of the Duke of Orléans, the Duke of Chartres, who was about 19 years old. Because of the desertion of the son of the Duke of Orléans, all the Bourbons remaining in France including the Duke of Orléans, were arrested April 5, 1793. The Duke remained in prison until October, during the Reign of Terror. He was tried on November 6, found guilty, and guillotined on that Sunday. Thus, Saint-Georges had lost a friend and a rich protector who, as it will be shown, he would have need later. With the defection of the Duke's son, all but Mme de Montesson were gone from this noble family of friends.

Dumouriez arresting the Commissioners

Dumouriez needed a base of operations and decided to take the city of Lille. He tried to recruit the troops in that city to aid in his plan, but they refused. At eight a.m., he ordered General Miaczynski to seize Lille. Saint-Georges was already in Lille at that time for the very purpose of protecting the city. When he learned of the plan, Saint-Georges rode full speed with Dumas, to Lille. He arrived in Lille at 10 o'clock in the morning and immediately revealed Dumouriez's plan to General Duval, who was in command of the district. Miaczynski was arrested at noon,. Lille was saved from Dumouriez and his criminal plans, thanks to the swiftness and heroism of Saint-Georges and his lieutenant colonel, Dumas. Although Saint-Georges was friendly with the house of Orléans, he did not compromise what he felt was his duty to his ideals regarding the revolution. None of his men had taken part in this treason of which he could be proud.

Saint-Georges' heroism and bravery were soon forgotten. Because of his connection with the house of Orléans, he was still under suspicion. During this time, everyone at one time or another was under suspicion. Also, because of the contrasts of his style of living from that of his troops and of his refined language, there was jealousy. Saint-Georges continued to dress well and kept a fine carriage of horses. He was suspected of lying, of embezzling funds from his squadron, and of sacrificing the needs of his men to his own personal needs. He was accused of having lived in luxury, that he had spent only a small portion of the money for his Legion on his troops and had spent the rest to pay his debts and to continue to live in luxury.

On May 2, 1793, the Commissioner Dufrenne wrote: "Saint-Georges is a man who will bear watching." Despite these accusations, in early July, he was confirmed in his rank of colonel by the executive committee and allowed to remain at the head of the 13th Regiment of Chasseurs (Hunters). He retained command of his corps until September 25, 1793, when the Executive Committee dismissed him. He felt betrayed and that this dismissal was totally unfounded and unjust. He wrote a letter to Minister Bouchotte to demand justice. The letter said:

> Until this time, I have waited submissively for you to inform me of the reasons which may have caused my suspension of duty; I can no longer wait in this cruel uncertainty; I feel entirely above reproach; I have at all times and places given proof of my citizenship and Republican sentiments, which are innate in one.

> Do me the grace, Citizen Minister, of allowing me to justify the false accusations which have been made against me, or to prove that your good faith has been betrayed; I beseech you in the name of humanity to grant me this justice, which is due every French Republican.

> I am, with sentiments of the most perfect good citizenship, your fellow-citizen.

Saint-Georges
Brigade Captain

The suspension was not lifted. I have no record that he was even answered. Saint-Georges wrote another letter that it seems, he sent to all the Presidents of the sections of Paris. The letter begins:

"Monsieur le President,

Saint-Georges, whose patriotism is recognized since the time of the Revolution, because of his conduct at Lille in Flanders (French Flanders) where he resided two years and where he commanded a company of National Guardsmen which he left only to serve as a volunteer aide-de-camp of M. M. Duhon and Miaczynski, which company co-jointly with all citizens will vouch for his patriotism, accepted the command of the hussards of the midi (South) desiring to continue and to prove his great worth through his valor and his enthusiasm for freedom, being unable to prove his zeal and assure success only with a pure body approved by the different sections whose civism he cherishes, hopes to be seconded by them, wishing to approve or disapprove the enrollments which he will have the honor to address to them successively.

> He has the humor to be,
> Monsieur le President,
> > Your very humble
> > And very obedient servant,
> > Saint-Georges"

In September of 1793 two accounts from the police in the National Archives qualifies him as "counter-revolutionary" and an "accomplice of Dumouriez and Miaczynski," although he had been a friend a short time earlier for renouncing Dumouriez as a traitor. On October, 1793, he was arrested and imprisoned first at Houdainville, then at Clermont-sur-Oise where he remained for almost a year.

Saint-Georges was fortunate that he was still alive, for people accused of similar crimes were most often guillotined. The Reign of Terror was still a part of daily life. Everyone was suspicious of everyone else and the suspicions usually ended with the loss of someone's head.

Several people came to Saint-Georges' defense trying to help redeem his good name. Some admitted that their suspicions had proven false. Even the 13th Regiment of Chasseurs or the Legion-Saint-Georges came to his defense by declaring that:

> Saint-Georges had completed his duties perfectly as a patriot and that they regretted that they missed this 'good chief' who had 'brought to the highest degree the love of his comrades.

He was released on October 23, 1794 by the Committee of Public Safety but he was not restored to the command of his troops. While he was away, the regiment had been under the command of a new officer, Target, who wanted very much to help restore the regiment to Saint-Georges' command. He wrote to Saint-Georges this touching letter:

"Target, temporary brigade captain of the 13th Regiment of Cavalry-Huntsman, to the Republican Saint-Georges, first brigade captain and founder of the Regiment.

As I have had the misfortune of being the passive and involuntary tool of the injustice done to you, it is my honor and my duty to properly repair it.

If I command the regiment you formed, I did not know the regiment well. But owing the honor only to your fall from grace, I think that I can only make myself worthy of the post that I have accepted in your absence by giving it back to him to whom it should still belong.

I therefore declare, on my gentleman's sword that my most fervent desire is to return to you a command which should never have been taken away and if I have been able to serve in some minor way the Regiment and my Country, I

now ask only as reward to serve
under your orders in whatever rank
that might be.

Target, Soissons 28th
Ventôse[i], third
Republican year, March 17,
1795"

Saint-Georges was encouraged by this letter and wrote another letter addressing a new petition to the Committee of Public Safety.

He called attention to the fact that he had been one of the first to make known the treason of Dumouriez; and he sent many documents which testified that he was a loyal gentleman and citizen. The mayor and municipal officials of Lille stated positively:

that the corps commanded by
Saint-Georges numbered only good
patriots in its ranks; they regret that
the Republic should have thought
it needed to deprive herself of the
services of so fine a citizen; and
the ex-colonel's comrades pay the
liveliest tributes to his bravery and
his qualities as a commander.

Saint-Georges' removal was assuredly nothing less than an arbitrary measure, as unjust as it was unjustified. With the preponderance of evidence in his favor, the Committee of Public

[i]Ventôse – 6th month in the French Revolutionary Calendar (from Feb 20th to March 21st)

Safety reinstated Saint-Georges to the command of the American Hussards on the 15th of May, 1795.

However, Saint-Georges had some new problems. During his absence the Regiment had been reorganized twice, first by Target and then by a M. Bouquet. Therefore, Saint-Georges became the third colonel. Target immediately stepped down, and the rivalry between Saint-Georges and Bouquet began. The situation became chaotic with two colonels giving orders. The Regiment became divided between the Saint-Georgists and the Bouquetistes.

Since the Regiment was originally Saint-Georges', the military Commission preferred him to Bouquet, especially since his commandment had been taken away form him by an arbitrary decision.

Bouquet took advantage of the fact that Saint-Georges had stayed in Paris and that while he was giving direct commands to the Regiment, Saint-Georges was seen as creating disorganization by trying to command without being present.

The situation grew worse for Saint-Georges when the Commune of Arras complained that the 13th Regiment had displayed royalist opinions. This accusation was so dangerous that it even affected Bouquet.

Again Saint-Georges lost his command! But again he was placed at the head of the squad by General Kermorvan to show that from then on he had the command of this unity.

Finally, politics entered and Saint-Georges was dismissed again on October 30, 1795 and Bouquet became commander of the 13th Regiment de Chasseurs à Cheval (13th Regiment of Horse Hunters).

This last dismissal was based on a certain article 15 of the decree of the third brumaire[ii] year IV (October 24, 1795). This article was replaced a year later on December 4, 1796.

Again Saint-Georges requested that the decision of dismissal be reconsidered. He wrote a letter to Rewbell presenting his case:

> George, Chef de Brigade du
> 13 Regiment de Chasseurs à cheval.
> To citizen Rewbell, one of the
> members of the executive directory.
> Citizen,
> I commanded the 13th
> Regiment of Hunters from the time
> of its creation; relieved of this
> position September 29, '93 by the
> Minister Bouchotte,
> I was reinstated the 24 Flored
> of the year III (May 15, 1794). But
> an act of the 8 Brumaire (October
> 29) following stated that:
> As I am included in Article
> 15 of the law of the 3rd day of the
> month of Brumaire (October 24),
> I am obliged to leave the 13th
> Regiment of Huntsmen (Cavalry)
> and to retire from every other
> commune than that in which the
> Regiment is presently placed.
> The above mentioned
> Article 15 is precisely one of those
> replaced by the law of the 14th

Brumaire of the year 5 (December 4, 1796) of which I am enclosing a copy.

I have constantly proven my attachment to the Revolution. I served it from the beginning of the war with a tireless zeal which even persecutions were not able to diminish. My only resource is to be reinstated in my rank. I address you with confidence, Citizen Director, and I demand of your spirit of justice the position of brigade captain of which I was deprived by virtue of an article which is no longer in effect since it was replaced by a subsequent law.

Greetings and respect
George.

His request was never answered and Saint-Georges' military career came to a sad and tragic end. Saint-Georges was not just fighting for his honor and for redress alone, he needed the position because he needed the money. The Revolution had taken its toll: many lost all they had; Saint-Georges was not excluded.

[1]Odet Denys explains in his book Article 15 and its relation to Saint-Georges. The explanation is long and a little complicated, but it can help understand the politics and paranoia that exists during any revolution and in this particular case, The French Revolution.

Article 15 which was brought against Saint-Georges was to suspend officers and commissaries of war who not being in activity of service the 15th germinal[iii] an III (April 5, 1795), had been placed from that time until the 14th thermidor[iv] of the same year (August 2, 1795). Saint-Georges was precisely not in action the 15th germinal year III (April 7, 1795) and had been re-integrated the following month, so that he did not fall under Article 15.

But this article appears at first glance, to have no connections other than dispositions of the decree of 3rd brumaire year IV (October 24, 1795).

Taken on the eve of the last session of the Convention, the decree in effect was directed against individuals capable of 'having provoked or signed seditious measures contrary to the laws in the primary or electoral assemblies,' on the other hand against immigrants, their relatives

[iii]Germinal – 7th month of the French Revolutionary Calendar (From March 22nd to April 22nd)

[iv]Thermidor – 11th month of the French Revolutionary Calendar (From July 19th to Aug 17th)

or allies, as well as by priests who had refused to support the revolution.

Those they wanted to reach were bourgeois, who had taken the part, sometimes even resulting in violence, against the decree which maintained in the next legislature body two-thirds of the members of the convention.

Article 15 hit, also, officers, war commissaries, employees of military administrators who, being in active service on the tenth of August, 1792, had retired since that date, then taking up service again in the army. Those were not only suspended but their job was taken away from them without the chance of being reinstated. So it was obviously a question of royalist soldiers, or supposedly royalist soldiers.

But concerning officers and war commissaries who were brought into question by article 15- -the one which concerned Saint-Georges a particular period (that of the fifth of August and the 2nd of April, 1795) was specified.

By what motives?

The answers given by events which preceded the 13th vendémiaire[v] (October 5, 1795) and by the reaction which followed this famous date, the beginning of the dazzling career of Bonaparte.

Since the fall of Robespierre, and particularly since the spring of 1795, there were many immigrants who had come back into the capitol.

They had allied themselves with a certain number of rich bourgeois, who were dissatisfied with the ruling regime and especially with the accelerating fall of the assignats; they had also taken contacts with some of the members of the convention who were very anxious to make a profitable change.

But if the period from April 5th to August 2, 1795 was specified, it's because during that period the ministry of war had been administered by one of the authors of the fall of Roberspierre, certainly, by Thermidorien[vi], as like the other people in power at the time, but whom the majority of

---

[vi]Thermidorien – Revolutionaries of the 9th Thermidor.

[v]Vendemiaire – First month in the French Revolutionary Calendar (from Sept 22nd/23rd/24th to Oct 21st/22nd/23rd)

the other thermidoriens had found,
at the date of this decree of the
3rd brumaire year IV (October 24,
1795), 'reactionary,' too zealous
not to be suspected of connivance
with the royalist or the federalists.

By taking this decree,
the convention, most of whose
members wanted to stay in power,
showed that they had not forgotten
to guard the days of before the
repression of the 13th vendémiare,
nor the role that certain officers had
played in the plot.

Because he had been reintegrated during this period,
Saint-Georges found himself among the mass of suspects. Yet
his dossier contained authentic proofs of good service given
before to the republic. And the texts stated that in this case his
suspension should be lifted. Yet it was not.

Once again, it definitively appears that he was the
victim of envious rivalries and of vigilant friendships. In any
hypotheses, the silence given to his request cannot be excused,
since the text by which he was dismissed was not found or had
been retracted.

It is obvious that Saint-Georges was certainly a victim
of politics; however, it was a time of politics. But he was more
fortunate than many accused of lesser crimes, who were not
fortunate enough to go to prison but instead were taken quickly
to the guillotine to loose their heads. Such was the fate of the
Duke of Orléans and so many lesser-known people with much
less influence or power. Many, in order to escape this fate, fled

the country to live in exile; others were ordered to leave or were forced into exile. It would not have been unusual at all had Saint-Georges suffered any of these other fates. It was not unusual that he was sent to prison on suspicions.

All letters in this chapter are in the National Archives of Paris, 1789-1799.

[1]Denys, Odet Qui était Le Chevalier de Saint-Georges n.p.

Chapter VI

Seeking a New Life
Toussaint L'Ouverture and The Haitian Revolution.

With the end of his military career, the death and exile of most of his friends and associates and having lost his money in the Revolution, the world looked very bleak for Saint-Georges. What would he do now? What could he do? He was well into his fifties, not a young man any longer, although he was still well built and handsome. With a torn Achilles tendon and his advanced age, fencing exhibitions did not appeal to him. What was he going to do?

From a point of desperation came a great idea. He would return to San Domingo and see if he could claim the plantation that his father had left behind. Perhaps in this way, he could sell it or get money from it in. At least it was property, and it presented a chance, a hope to recover.

Saint-Georges left for San Domingo. Before the ship could dock, on the horizon, he could see smoke and hear explosions. What was happening? Saint-Georges had not kept in touch with the situation on this island or he would have known what to expect.

There, taking place before him was another Revolution, but very different in its causes and in its execution. This was an armed uprising of the slaves and former slaves against the whites. And it was not a different ruler who was desired but a completely different system. Here, freedom was the issue, freedom from slavery.

Christopher Columbus discovered Haiti and found that the Indians there had already settled it. They were peaceful and helped Columbus and his men. In the name of Spain, Columbus annexed the island, and called it Hispañiola, and immediately began exploiting the natives. They introduced Christianity, forced labor in mines, murder, rape, bloodhounds, strange diseases and artificial famine (by the destruction of cultivation to starve the rebellious). These and other requirements of the higher civilization reduced the native population from an estimated half-a-million, perhaps a million, to 60,000 in 15 years. Since the population of Indians was being wiped out, there was a fear of a shortage of forced labor. The Spanish decided to take slaves from Africa. Thus, in 1517, Spain started the slave trade business in America.

Later, France gained the western part of this island through a treaty. In order to supplement the labor force on its part of the island, France brought in whites who were like the indentured servants in North America, who could work for a period of time and gain their freedom. They also had freedmen from France, who were offered property if they would work the property for 36 months. These people were known as les trente-six mois. The whites found the climate too hot. More slaves were needed, thus the number of slaves imported increased to thousands brought to the Americas.

I won't go into the well-known details of the cruelty of the "middle passage." Eventually millions of slaves were brought to the other islands in the West Indies and to America.

Slavery in San Domingo was conducted more brutally than in America as I previously stated. This among many other reasons led to resistance and finally insurrection. C. L. R. James in his book, The Black Jacobins gives us a description of the conditions of the slave in San Domingo. He says:

> The difficulty was that though one could trap them like an animal, transport them in pens, work them alongside an ass or a horse and beat both with the same stick, stable them and starve them, they remained, despite their black skins and curly hair, quite invincibly human beings; with the intelligence and resentments of human beings. To cow them into the necessary docility and acceptance necessitated a regime of calculated brutality of property-owners apparently careless of preserving their property; they first had to ensure their own safety.[1]

He goes on to describe in detail the types of torture inflicted on the slaves for the least fault:

---irons on the hands and feet, blocks of wood that the slaves had to drag behind them wherever they went, the tin-plate mask designed to prevent the slaves from eating the sugar-cane, the iron collar. Whipping was interrupted in order to pass a piece of hot wood on the buttocks of the victim; salt, pepper, citron, cinders, aloes, and hot ashes were poured on the bleeding wounds. Mutilations were common, limbs, ears, and sometimes the private parts, to deprive them of the pleasures they could indulge in without expense. Their masters poured burning wax on their arms and hands and shoulders, emptied the boiling cane sugar over their heads, burned them alive, roasted them on slow fires, filled them with gun powder and blew them up with a match; buried them up to the neck and smeared their heads with sugar that the flies might devour them; fastened them near to nests of ants or wasps; made them eat their excrement, drink their urine, and lick the salava of other slaves. One colonists was known in moments of anger to throw himself on his

slaves and stick his teeth into their
flesh.[2]

These were not isolated events. These were commonly
practiced daily, to perfection. Enough said about the civilized
Europeans. Do they seem like the same people with whom
Saint-Georges was dining, hunting and dancing? Well, not
exactly, these island whites were their emissaries.

All the slaves were not treated in this fashion. There
was a small privileged group or caste composed of the foremen
of the gangs, coachmen, cooks, butlers, maids, nurses, female
companions, and other house-servants. These same people in
America were called "house-Niggers." Because of their better
treatment and small privileges, they were very faithful to their
masters, many being spies and anti-black. C. L. R. James
described them in this way:

> Permeated with the vices of
> their masters and mistresses, these
> upper servants gave themselves
> airs and despised the slaves in the
> fields. Dressed in cast-off silks and
> brocades, they gave balls in which,
> like trained monkeys, they danced
> minuets, and bowed and curtseyed
> in the fashion of Versailles. But a
> few of these used their position to
> cultivate themselves, to gain a little
> education, to learn all they could.[3]

Among those of this caste were found some of the future
leaders of San Domingo. Toussaint Bréda, later Toussaint
L'Ouverture (the liberator of San Domingo) belonged to this

caste as did Henri Christophe, who became the Emperor of Haiti and Dessalines, the first Emperor of Haiti.

As early as 1685 or perhaps before, every Mulatto was free, up to the age of 24. This created a third group or caste. The house servants or the caste formally mentioned were still slaves although treated better than the others. The Mulattoes had white blood and most were free. There was no law, but since the masters did not want to increase the number of their enemies, they sought to align the Mulattoes with the whites. The Negro Code in 1685, in San Domingo, authorized marriage between the white and the slave who had children by him. This marriage ceremony freed the slave and her children. The Code gave the free Mulattoes and the free Negroes equal rights with the whites.

This was before the birth of Saint-Georges in Guadeloupe which may account for his and his mother's situation, since racial prejudice was not as great at that time as it became later.

The Mulattoes served another useful purpose to the whites. Since there was a shortage of women and since most of the white women sent to San Domingo were the ugliest and the lowest of France, the Mulatto women served additional purpose.

> The Mulatto women lived in such comfort and luxury that in 1789, of 7000 Mulatto women in San Domingo, 5000 were either prostitutes or were kept as mistresses of white men.[4]

The degree of freedom of the Mulatto changed constantly according to the whims of their masters, individually and sometimes collectively. In spite of this capriciousness, the Mulattoes, after many years, owned property and amassed much wealth, while at the same time growing to outnumber the whites.

The Mulattoes and freed Negroes also became slave owners and later shared with the whites the support of the institution of slavery and the disdain for the slave. They became rich enough to send their children to France to become educated and became money lenders to the whites. Their position was unique in that they could not be white or fully accepted as equal to whites, and they did not wish nor did they associate themselves with these barbarous, ignorant slaves. The more freedom, wealth and education they attained, the more frustrated they became. The Mulatto, rather than be a slave to a black, would have killed himself.

After 1789, and the taking of the Bastille, the Mulattoes, as well as the slaves saw that they had something in common with the French peasants and that maybe now, there would be a change in policy in San Domingo, like the one happening in France.

There was a movement in France for the abolition of slavery in San Domingo by a group known as "The Friends of the Negro." Their influence and interest fluctuated for several years, and as a result, the situation of the Mulattoes was the most frustrating. They were always considered first when the issue of abolition was discussed. They were talked about as being human beings and the slaves as property.

This constantly changing position of the Mulattoes caused them to band together in large numbers with their wealth and education. Such groups represented a great concern for the white slave-owners, who did not want the Mulattoes to unite and lead the Negroes into insurrection. But a small number of whites or small landowners still showed no respect to the Mulatto and with little provocation, attacked and lynched them.

The Mulattoes constantly made demands for their rights and entered into many agreements with the whites for their rights, in return for a promise to help keep the Negroes as slaves. But these agreements were always broken.

> Rejected in France, humiliated at home, the Mulattoes organized a revolt. It was a quarrel between bourgeoisie and monarchy that brought the Paris masses on the political stage. It was the quarrel between whites and Mulattoes that woke the sleeping slaves.[5]

The same Raymond who had asked the assembly to form a corps of blacks to fight for the French Revolution that was lead by Saint-Georges was now speaking again, stating that: "Mulattoes must be given rights so as to unite with whites to keep down the slaves." The compromise was made but later broken, as was the pattern.

There had begun slave uprisings that were taking small tolls on the lives of whites and their property. Although what was needed was a great unifying leader, these uprisings caused great concern. The man who was to eventually lead the masses was just now joining the slaves. He was a leader from the very beginning because he had natural leadership qualities, even though he was forty-nine years old and could scarcely read and write, and spoke terrible French.

The Mulattoes, for more promises of equal rights, volunteered to fight against the revolting slaves. They were used and again discarded. The Mulattoes, tired of persecution, revolted. They were lead by Rigaud, a trained soldier who had fought in the American Revolution and Beauvais, whose family had been free and rich, and Pinchinot, the politician. They demanded complete equality. If not, they threatened civil war. Again the whites agreed. Six days later, all rights were withdrawn. There followed much fighting and destruction of white property. So now the Mulattoes were fighting the whites, and the slaves were fighting the whites. Fighting was almost everywhere; in some provinces, blacks were leading Mulattoes and in others, Mulattoes were leading blacks with some well-meaning whites thrown in. Destruction, violence and cruelty were the norm. But since the former slaves were destroying the plantations, etc., they were also making it difficult to survive. They were not making progress at winning a war and taking over the country; they were hungry. Fearing that they could not continue and would be eventually defeated, the leaders, Jean-François, Biassou and Toussaint tried to make a deal with the Assembly. They offered to turn against their brothers and bring them back where they belonged, in bondage, for a promise of freedom and political rights for the leaders. No one is perfect and with all the greatness in the life of Toussaint, this betrayal of his brothers must be remembered. The colonists refused the offer. Jean-François promised, "For the freedom of 400 of the leaders and forgetfulness of the past, he would lead the blacks back to slavery." The former slaves were bargained with for a moment and were asked to return the white prisoners as a sign of good faith. This was done but the Assembly again refused to grant freedom to the leaders. Toussaint tried to negotiate and even reduce the number to be freed and given

135

political rights from 400 to 60. The colonists literally laughed at him. Thereupon Toussaint made his decision to fight for the liberation of all slaves and mulattoes, a decision that he never changed. This occurred in 1792.

Toussaint began to train the ignorant blacks in the methods of war; he, as well as his army started from the beginning. By July, 1792, he had about 500 trained troops.

Most of the Mulattoes except Rigaud, who hated whites, were not in as complete a revolt as was Toussaint. They were still looking upon the slave revolt as a huge riot, which would be put down in time, once the division between the slave-owners was closed.

For the next few years, along with the Revolution in France, San Domingo was busy with many intrigues. The Mulattoes vacillated from one position to another. Toussaint and his rivals Jean-François and Biassou joined the Spanish in the Spanish part of the island. Jean-François and Biassou were happy at being armed by the Spanish to kill other whites. Toussaint was only using the Spanish, since he knew that they were trying to use him. He knew that if he helped them to defeat the French, they would eventually restore slavery.

San Domingo was the greatest prize of the French possessions, and it produced great wealth for many, including Saint-Georges' father. It was the richest island in the West Indies. The British along with the Spanish wanted this prize desperately. The Spanish already had a foothold. Now the British had an opportunity to get into the act.

The colonists and the Mulattoes who wanted the restoration of slavery, invited the British to help them regain their "property." The British did not want war with France and had not until this time tried to take the island. Now, however they were able to enter without repercussions. They were welcomed with open arms. It looked to be an easy task to take the island, since the forces there were so divided.

General Rigaud, Beauvais and Pinchinot were on the side of the French and Toussaint, Biassou and Jean-François were with the Spanish; the Spanish were actually allies of the British. In a short time, the British had captured most of the French part of the island. Troops sailing from Barbados captured Martinique, Saint Lucia, and Guadeloupe. The British were already plotting to deal with the Spanish.

Finally the Convention in Paris abolished all slavery in all the colonies.

> It declares that all men, without distinction of color, domicile in the colonies, are French citizens, and enjoy all the rights assured under the Constitution.

When the news reached San Domingo and Toussaint, he contacted the Governor of San Domingo, Laveaux, relating that he was ready to help the French. Laveaux, accepted his offer and made him a Brigadier General.

Toussaint started his assaults by first attacking his black brothers Biassou and Jean-François, who were content working with the Spanish, and added their troops to his army. Next, he attacked and completely demoralized the Spanish. Now, he was free to attack the British, which he did. Victory after victory, he began capturing most of the island from the British.

Toussaint, now a French officer, and in charge of an army of about 5000 men, held many strategic positions and continued to inflict losses on the British. In the South, Rigaud and his army contributed their share against the British.

"Helped by the climate, the black laborers so recently slaves, and the loyal mulattoes, led by their own officers, inflicted on Britain the severest defeat that has befallen British expeditionary force between the days of Elizabeth and the Great War. The full story remained hidden for over a century, until it was unearthed in 1906 by Fortescue, the historian of the British Army.[6]

> ---Yet they poured their troops into these pestilent islands, in the expectation that thereby they would destroy the power of France, only to discover, when it was too late, that they had practically destroyed the British Army.

Serving under Toussaint were such great soldiers as Dessalines, Henri Christophe, Paul L'Ouverture, his brother and Moïse, his adopted nephew.

Sometimes these troops were without food or adequate weapons. The British tried to find a weak spot, bribing them with offers of money, but with no success. However, the British were successful in paying other ignorant blacks to fight against Toussaint.

Spain and France made peace at the Treaty of Bale on July 22, 1795. Now Toussaint could concentrate more on the British who continued to pour money into the fighting behind the French slave-owners, mulatto slave-owners, and some freed blacks.

The British were losing badly but could not be completely driven out because the Mulattoes continued to conspire with them against Toussaint and the French. If the British were no real threat anymore, the Mulattoes were. The Mulattoes had property, and had received money from the British. Part of their property had been slaves, whom they wanted returned. Most Mulattoes who fought with Toussaint and the French, wanted an independent San Domingo with slavery, and planned to go to great lengths to bring about this situation.

Toussaint was not a brutal man. Whenever he captured the Mulattoes, he would ask only that they take an oath of allegiance to the Republic. Then, he would pardon them. As soon as his back was turned, they would conspire with the British and overturn his victories.

> ---they were the chief support of the British, who without them would have been driven out long before 1798. They caused Toussaint to lose many of his most important captures.[7]

Toussaint became very angry and stated that:

> Never have I experienced so many treasons. And I take an oath that henceforth I shall treat them in a manner very different to that which I have done hitherto. Whenever I have made them prisoners, I have treated them like a good father. The ungrateful wretches have replied by seeking to deliver me to our enemies.[8]

Later, a group of Mulattoes took Laveaux, the Governor of the island who was making his headquarters at LeCap, and put him in prison and named Villate, the new Governor of the island. Toussaint was enraged and sent Pierre Michel, one of his colonels, to march on LeCap. He also sent two divisions under the direction of Dessalines to LeCap. He arrived a few days later with his personal cavalry-guard but found that the situation was almost under control. Villate had fled with a small group of supporters. Shortly after, a group of black women heard some of Villate's soldiers insinuate that Laveaux had two ships in the harbor loaded with chains to throw the Negroes again into slavery. The black soldiers, who had supported and liberated Laveaux, surrounded him and were going to murder him. Toussaint again interrupted and saved Laveaux's life.

Laveaux realized how powerful Toussaint was and that he would still have problems with the Mulattoes, proclaimed Toussaint Assistant to the Governor, and swore that he would never do anything without consulting him. He called him the savior of constituted authority, the black Spartacus.

Laveaux was sure that Rigaud was also in the conspiracy with the other mulattoes. He felt that even with Toussaint, the colony was in danger, so he pleaded with the Minister in France to send troops and a Commission and "laws and all that is needed to make them respected."

The French government sent a Commission which landed at LeCap on May 11th, 1796. The Commission was composed of five men; Giraud, Leblanc, Roume, Sonthonax and Raymond, whom we remember again as the mulatto who had called for the forming of the corps that Saint-Georges commanded. According to Denys, it was with these men that Saint-Georges returned to San Domingo.

Although Saint-Georges was a mulatto, he was received with open arms by the blacks. And although these were difficult times, there were feasts held in his honor.

Saint-Georges took great caution to find the property of his father. When he finally found it, he discovered that it was deserted and, for want of up keeping, was over-run with weeds. Everything of value had been taken by one or more of the many armies which looted and burned everything they passed.

With nothing to be gained by staying, Saint-Georges, after a short time returned to Paris.

*For a complete history of San Domingo and the life of Toussaint L'Ouverture, see C. L. R. James book, The Black Jacobins.

---

[1]James, C.L.R. p.11

[2]Ibid. p.12

[3]Ibid. p.19

[4]Ibid. p.32

[5]Ibid. p.81

[6]Ibid. p.164

[7]Ibid. p.165

[8]Ibid. p.181

Chapter VII

Post Revolutionary Days in Paris

In Paris, Saint-Georges was a very disappointed and sad man. His trip had not been successful and seeing the fighting and killing did not please him at all.

The Revolution had brought about great changes in his beloved Paris. Since most of his friends and acquaintances were either dead or in exile, he was almost alone. There was a new class ruling in the social circles. The former aristocrats had their own problems. Saint-Georges was a forgotten man. He wandered around the City, like a foreigner, in this Paris which had made him famous.

There wasn't very much for him to do, but there was a new organization, Le Circle de L'Harmonie (The Circle of Harmony), which Saint-Georges joined to direct some concerts.

He reminisced about the old Paris in which he had lived, had entertained and had enjoyed so much. It was gone. Even with all of its faults, it had been the Paris of fêtes and balls and salons and a million other pleasurable diversions. In that Paris he made many friends and a few enemies. It had disappeared.

The old Paris had not been good to peasants, who worked hard, paid the taxes but could hardly improve their circumstances. But St.- Georges had cared and tried to make life better for a few. He was also aware that these negative things about Paris had helped to bring about the Revolution. What more could he have done? After all, he was not a man of politics nor of great power, just a humble mulatto trying to navigate the complicated French life, to produce and perform good music; to bring joy and pleasure to his life as well as to others.

He thought about the new Paris which had forgotten him. The poor still struggled with their survival and hoped that the Revolution would bring a better life. They had no time to concern themselves with him. That he understood.

He thought about how he was treated by the people in the streets who seemed to feel that he was not one of the oppressors and not one of them. They probably felt closer to him because of his color that put him a peg beneath the ruling class, and certainly a peg or two above them. They were also aware of his gentleness, and some knew of his generosity, which was not so common in the ruling class.

He thought about how he was received and treated by his contemporaries. He wondered if had he not been so gifted and talented, how would he have been received. Would they have accepted him just as a man, not a colored man; as a musician, not a multi talented musician? When one is loved, he thought, one does not always know why nor does one really care. To be admired, loved, and treated well is a pleasure. He knew that there were some who really cared for him and that his color, not his talent, made them care more. They were truly friends!

He remembered the many women who professed love for him. Some may have thought of him as a curiosity, but most really cared. After all, when he was with them, he gave them his undivided attention. He was gentle and caring. He believed that the women never felt used by him. He gave them all that he could give. He gave them pleasure, and they returned the deed. He regretted that he had never married or had children. He could have married a woman beneath his station but not one of noble birth. He remembered the rejections that he had received on several occasions when he was a young man. The message was clear. Odet Denys captures clearly the dilemma.

> A black man can marry a white woman if she occupies an inferior rank to his in society: she brings to him a dowry of prestige and the privileges of the whites, but he helps her to climb on the steps of the circus in which the human comedy is played.[1]

St.-Georges decided not to play that game. So, he was old and sick with no wife to care for him and no children to carry on his name and blood. After his great disappointment as a youth, he put away all thoughts of marriage. Now it was too late.

He thought of the advantages that one had in rising above his birth status. How the rich bourgeoisie could purchase positions and titles and pass them on to their children and how marriages could benefit in raising one to a higher position in the Paris of yesterday. He spoke of the Queen, Marie Antoinette, and how she and the King were very tolerant of the conduct of the people. There was a couplet sung by one of the peasants on the birth of her son. They consented to listen without displeasure.

Our charming Antoinette
Had a little fellow, just now,
And I seen the little Princes
Carpet tack.
It rose, and stood up.
I think it's going to be a real nail![2]

"Far from being offended by this familiarity, Louis XVI laughed heartedly. The queen did the same."

In Paris, Saint-Georges seemed to have lost his liveliness and his many interests. He just lived form day to day, seemingly without purpose. He now experienced a new kind of loneliness, the loneliness of being without many friends, without being invited to many functions, without the balls and the other fêtes. He knew the other loneliness, that of being lonely in the crowd. Now, he was practically alone. He did, however, have a few friends and acquaintances including Louise Fusil and his good friend La Motte, who helped to give life some purpose for him.

He had become very ill and complained of bladder pains. He sought no medical care and felt that it was not very serious. Later, when he became too ill to take care of himself and needed attention, Nicholas Duhamel, a former officer and friend from the regiment took him in to care for him. His strong, handsome body no longer resembled that of the great Saint- Georges. He seemed to have lost the will to live.

Saint-Georges never recovered to go back to his island country. On June 12, 1799, he died. An ulcer of the bladder had taken him away.

The death certificate stated; Saint-Georges Bologne instead of Bologne Saint-Georges, Joseph, 60 years old. The death certificate also gave the date of his birth, 1739.

Thus a great career had ended. This unusual, generous man died alone with no family and few friends. What a sad and tragic death, alone, without love! A man who had loved and had been loved by so many; a man who had brought so much joy to so many lives was gone.

His best friend La Motte wrote: "At his death, there was no knowledge of any family. His father had had a legitmate daughter...but I searched for her in vain. Perhaps she had emigrated, or perhaps she had died. So far as I know she had never had anything to do with her half brother...This man who was once so sought after...ended with only Duhamel and myself for companions."

For his tombstone, I will quote the final words of those who wrote of him before and from some of those who knew him.

Lionel De La Laurencie wrote:

> Thus disappeared one of the most curious and engaging figures of the dying eighteenth century. Saint-Georges was a remarkably gifted man, full of generosity and delicacy of feeling. Liberal and beneficent, he often deprived himself of the necessities of life in order to aid the unfortunate. His contemporaries use the expression 'full and soft' to express his violinist gifts, and, in truth, it really seems

to qualify his manner, in which the dual trends of his temperament are united, in a mingling of vivacity, brilliancy and dreamy melancholy. Since November 28, 1912, a street in Basse-Terre bears his name.[3]

From Henry Angelo came these words:

The Chevalier de Saint-Georges died at Paris, regretted by his friends, and by the few who knew how to feel for, or excuse, the imperfections of humanity---qualities from which none of us can hope to be exempt.

The following words come from an article taken from a Belgium Encyclopedia.

It has been regretted that Saint-Georges had not given a more solid direction to the talents with which he had been endowed by nature. He would have been able to play another role in the world, and yield recommendable to the less frivolous titles than those he had obtained. One eulogy we cannot refuse him, is his impartiality and benevolence. He deprived himself to relieve the unfortunate; and several needy old men were his boarders, as long as his faculties permitted him. He should be especially praised for never having taken undue advantage of his incomparable superiority in fencing.

The Larousse Grand Universal Dictionary paid this tribute:

> Let us repeat in finishing that the Chevalier de Saint-Georges distinguishes himself among the personage of his time, selfish and mischievous for the most part, by a generosity and a strength of character very rare. Until the end of his days he helped the poor and even had his special poor, that he supported completely.

R. Duchaussoy in his article Un Guadeloupéen Extraordinaire said:

> He left the memory of a man full of distinction, of a goodness going so far as to almost weakness, his character a little soft and in which his only ambition had been to love and to make himself loved.

E. M. von Arndt, the German poet who knew Saint-Georges very well wrote:

St.-Georges, the great George, died a few days after my arrival in Paris. St.-Georges, the representative of the French nation.....St. Georges was dead and so great was public interest that the news made people forget the battles of Verona and Stochart. All the day, they talked about nothing else but that. In all the theatres, promenades, cafes and gardens resounded the name of the great, the amiable St.-Georges. In the streets, they stopped to exchange the news. For three days, four days, his name echoed in all the newspapers. They lauded his skill in all the arts, his fine manner, his force, his generosity and gaiety, and generally concluded with these words:" 'He was the perfect Frenchman, that is to say, the most amiable of mortals. He was the Voltaire of equitation, music, dancing and skill in the use of weapons.'

In truth, St.-Georges is an astonishing figure in the eyes of a German, whose education is so silly that he considers skill in bodily exercises as one of the little supplementary things of life. St.-

Georges was the handsomest, the strongest and the most agreeable man of his times. He was a fateful friend, a good citizen, a man of society, full of so many charms and virtues that any single one of them would have caused us to mourn his death. He was the Alciabides of his time, he loved pleasure, but never abused it. Oh! such marvelous gifts merit immortality and a people with a keen and ever ready recognition of beauty as the French, will admire him eternally.

Allan Bradley said: "There were certainly greater composers than Saint-Georges during the late 18th century but none who possessed anywhere near his remarkable range of talents, his exotic persona and fascinating personality. He was a man."

And finally his countryman and biographer Odet Denys.

In his honor, let us remember that the fever of pleasures did not succeed in drying up his heart; his glory did not make him lose his mind and spirit. The noise of the cymbals did not prevent him from hearing the gentle voice of his soul. He kept until his last breath a simple and good nature.

He was horrified at the idea of hurting someone when the lively character which is considered a part of people from the island had for a moment won over his usual affability, then right away he regretted having acted that way and tried in a thousand ways to erase his wrong doings. It was especially remarkable when he became ill; he deprived himself to be able to continue to help them. He helped them until he had completely used up his own means, until he used up his own strength.

---

[1]Deny's Odet.

[2]unknown

[3]Lionel De La Laurencie: <u>Musical Quarterly</u> n.p.

Postlude

I hope I have succeeded in giving an accurate and as penetrating view of the life of Saint-Georges as is possible with what may seem to be much information but is in fact very little, especially about certain periods of his life and more definitive information about his amours. It would have been an easy matter if Saint-Georges had written his memoirs which was common for men of his position and social status of that time in history.

His life was so fascinating and his talents so refined and prodigious. The fact that he was black made his life even more incredible and interesting. He was the only black man of his time, except for General Alexandre Dumas, who lived the life of a nobleman and was accepted in the highest places. General Dumas was born in 1762, and as previously stated, was the father of Alexandre Dumas, père, the author of The Three Musketeers, The Count of Monte Cristo, and many other classics. Saint-Georges died at the end of what has been called the Revolutionary Period which, ended officially in 1799, the same year of his death. Dumas père lived in a new and different Paris. The social life was still the Parisian life but the country had undergone great changes. It was now the Paris of Napoleon Bonaparte and his lovely wife, Josephine.

Saint-Georges was almost forgotten in history, except for Roger de Beauvoir's book in 1740, and Odet Denys' book in 1972. Strangely, with all the material available now on Saint-Georges' life, Denys' book is never mentioned.

France rediscovered Saint-Georges in the late nineties. A street was named for him in Paris in December of 2001. On March 6, 2003, CBC television, "Opening Night," in Paris, presented a TV documentary entitled, "Le Mozart Noir: Reviving a Legend." Also, there is a bust of Saint-Georges in Guadeloupe, his birthplace. When I visited Guadeloupe twenty years ago, hardly anyone had heard of him. CD's of most of his compositions can now be purchased on line from France.

The plaque over the street in Paris honoring Saint-Georges

The bust of Saint-Georges in Guadeloupe

Bibliography

Angelo's Pic-Nic or Table Talk, Illustrated by G. Cruikshank, London 1834

Angelo: The Reminiscences of Henry Angelo, Paris 1830

Arndt, E.M. Von Bruchstücke einer durch Frankreich im Fruhling und Sommer, Vol. II,

Beauvoir, Roger de: Le Chevalier de Saint-Georges, 1840 Paris, H.L. Delloye

Bénéfices d'inventaires, Paris 1775

Brook, Barry S.: La Symphonie Française dans la seconde moité du XVIIIe siècle

Bernard Miall: Pierre Garat, Singer and Exquisite, His life and his World, 1762-1823 London, 1913

Bradley, Alan: Le Chevalier de Saint-Georges (1748-1799)

C.L.R. James: The Black Jacobins. Vintage Books. 1963 Alfred A. Knoff, Inc. and Random House, Inc.

Daressy: Archives des Maîtres d'Armes de Paris, 1888

Distinguished Negroes Abroad

Encyclopedia Larousse du Xxe Siècle Vol. 6

Early Negro Musicians, n.d. n.p.

Bourgeois, Gaston: Le Chevalier de Saint-Georges, Inexactitudes Commises par See biographies. 1949 Paris n.p.

Gossec, F. S D'Anvers, Paris 1764

Grétry: Mémoires, ou Essai sur la Musique

Grimm, Diderot, Raynal, Meister et autres: Correspondence littéraire, philosophique et critique, Vols. 11, 12, 15 Paris 1776 n.p.

J.A. Rogers: World's Great Men of Color, Vol. II. published 1947, renewed 1925

J. Buchan Telfer: The Chevalier d'Eon de Beaumont, published 1885, Paris

La Boëssière: Traité de l'art des armes, Paris 1818

Larousse: Grand Dictionnaire Universel du 19e siècle, Vol. 14, Paris 1875

Thiébault, Paul-Charles François: Mémoires 1816 n.p.

Lewis Wade Jones: Nuggets from World History, copyright, 1933, Chevalier de Saint-Georges

Lionel de La Laurencie: Musical Quarterly (Schirmer's) Boston n.d. n.p.
The Chevalier de Saint-Georges, violinist, January, 1919, Boston. n.p.

Louis Dufrane: Gossec, Sa Vie, Ses Oeuvres, Paris

M. Gaston-Leon Bourgeois: Un Enfant Célèbre de la Guadeloupe, Le Chevalier de Saint-Georges.

Marjorie Corny: The Chevalière d'Eon, London, 1932

Mémoires du Général de Marbot, Paris

Mémoires de Bachaument

Le Mercure de France, April, 1772

Michaud, Biographie Universelle (see "St. Georges")

Michaud: Biographie Universelle (see "Saint-Georges"). Paris

Odet Denys: Qui était Le Chevalier de Saint-Georges. (1739-1799)? Paris 1972

M. de la Fontelle: La vie militaire, politique et privée

Omnibus of French Literature, Vol. 1-Steinhaven and Walter.

Pierre Groslande: L'Université Française (Le Chevalier de Saint-Georges).

Pincherle, Marc: Jean-Marie Leclair, L'ainé

Prud'homme: Jacques Gabriel François: Joseph Gossec, 1734 la vie, les oeuvres, l'homme et l'artiste

R. Duchaussoy: Un Guadeloupéen Extraordinaire, Le Chevalier de Saint-Georges.

About The Author

Walter Smith was born and raised in Durham, North Carolina, where he attended North Carolina Central University, majoring in French. There, he was a member of the Phi Beta Sigma Fraternity. After graduation, he moved to New York City. He taught French and Spanish in the NYC Public Schools for several years. Later he attended graduate school at Laval University, in Quebec, Canada.

Having written a few short stories, he moved to Los Angeles to try writing for television. After only nine months, he was fortunate enough to land an assignment to write an episode of the popular TV show, *Good Times*. Over the next few years, he wrote a story for the sit-com, *Different Strokes*, which was nominated for the Humanitas Award, and later, a story for *Magnum P.I.* He is a member of the Writers Guild of America and currently teaches high school French in Lynwood, California.